Pas

Cookbook

This Book Includes:

Sauces and Homemade Pasta

Cookbook.

The Complete Recipe Book to

Cook the Most Delicious and

Tasty Italian Dishes

Owen Conti

Legal & Disclaimer

The information contained in this book and its contents is not designed to replace or take the place of any form of medical or professional advice; and is not meant to replace the need for independent medical, financial, legal or other professional advice or services, as may be required. The content and information in this book has been provided for educational and entertainment purposes only.

The content and information contained in this book has been compiled from sources deemed reliable, and it is accurate to the best of the Author's knowledge, information and belief. However, the Author cannot guarantee its accuracy and validity and cannot be held liable for any errors and/or omissions. Further, changes are periodically made to this book as and when needed. Where appropriate and/or necessary, you must consult a professional (including but not limited to your doctor, attorney, financial advisor or such other professional advisor) before using any of the suggested remedies, techniques, or information in this book.

Table of Contents:

Homemade Pasta Cookbook

Pasta Sauces Cookbook

10

Homemade Pasta Cookbook

A Recipe Book for Beginners to Master the Art of Handmade Italian Pasta

Owen Conti

Introduction

When most people think of Italian recipes, pasta comes into their mind. Pasta has traditionally been an Italian recipe but it has become a popular recipe all over the world. It is a common site to see many Americans enjoying pasta recipes in an Italian restaurant.

While many people love pasta, only a few of them know how to prepare them. Many people think it is complicated to make them while it is very easy.

It is essential for having the right pasta machine when you want to prepare homemade pasta.

Pasta combines well with meat stews, vegetables and vegetable salads, and with almost any soup or sauce, without diminishing the taste, or appeal of the pasta accompaniment, but instead enhancing it.

Pasta can also easily be served to enhance the appeal of the meal and will blend in well with almost any type of garnish.

Importantly are the minimal ingredients required to prepare the dough and the commonality of the ingredients.

With some practice, fresh pasta making, should thus be a shared endeavor in your meal planning and pasta should become an ever so often meal you could prepare, for special occasions, to entertain guests and the family or simply just treat yourself to a delicious meal.

Nutritionally, pasta is mainly carbohydrates, i.e., starch, with some protein and manganese. However, kinds of pasta may contain some additions such as spinach, herbs spices, cheeses, mushrooms and various other seasonings. The net effect of these additions being to enhance the nutrition composition of the pasta, improving the nutrient contents by incorporating, vitamins, iron and other minerals found in the added ingredients.

Pasta is one of the most popular meals enjoyed by millions, no, billions of people around the world. Pasta is indeed delicious and popular around the world with almost every corner of the globe customizing a pasta recipe and enjoying it by the cultural practice of that region.

This book contains information about Italian pasta and how to prepare them. It has Italian pasta recipes categorized into short, long and stuffed pastas. There is also information on how to prepare the dough to make pasta. As you may know, the dough-making process is fundamental in making pasta.

Many of us cannot enjoy a great tasting pasta dish unless the pasta is cooked to perfection each time. If you fit into this category, don't worry—this book the perfect directions to make the ideal and tender pasta with every recipe that you make.

All recipes included in the book will only be for homemade pasta. At the same time, for cooking and sauces, Owen Conti has made another book titled Pasta Sauce Cookbook and is available on Amazon.

Chapter 1: The Various Types of Italian Pasta Dough

Gluten-Free Pasta Dough

Cook Time: 45 Minutes

Serves: 4

Difficulty: Difficult

Ingredients:

- 150 g gluten-free rice flour , plus more to dust
- ¼ teaspoon fine sea salt
- 1 tablespoon extra-virgin olive oil
- 1 tablespoon cornflour
- 2 tablespoons xanthan gum
- 50 g potato starch

- 3 large eggs

Preparation:

1. Process all the ingredients in a food processor to create rough dough. Dust the working surface with flour and place the dough there. Knead until the dough is smooth.

2. Divide the dough into four and then use your fingertips to press each piece. Put into a pasta machine to roll. Begin with the widest setting and then turn again.

3. Roll the pasta twice on each setting, apart from the two narrowest settings, to form a 2mm thick sheet. Place the pasta on surface dusted with flour and use a dump tea towel to cover it. Proceed for the other dough.

4. Transform the dough into pasta of your choice. Making tagliatelle, roll the pasta on that setting on the machine. You can alternatively use a knife to into strips of 7mm and put on a surface dusted with flour.

Nutritional value per serving:

Calories 273, Fats 8.1 g, Saturates 1.7 g, Sugars 0.3 g, Protein 8.9 g, Carbs 41.3 g

Fresh Egg Pasta Dough

Cook time: 30 Minutes

Serves 4

Difficulty: Medium

Ingredients:

- 600 g Tipo '00' flour
- 6 large eggs

Preparation:

1. Pour the flour on a pasta board. Make a fountain and the middle and crack in the eggs.

2. Beat the eggs using a fork until smooth. Thoroughly mix with flour.

3. Dust with flour and knead to form a silky, smooth and elastic dough.

4. Use a cling film to cover the dough and allow 30 minutes to rest in a refrigerator.

5. Roll it and shape it the way you want.

Nutritional value per serving:

Calories 620, Fats 12 g, Saturates 3 g, Sugars 2.2 g, Protein 26.7 g, Carbs 101.4 g, Fiber 3.9 g

Royal Pasta Dough

Cook time: 30 minutes

Serves: 8

Difficulty: Not too tricky

Ingredients:

- 12 large free-range eggs

- 2 tablespoons extra virgin olive oil

- 75 g fine semolina

- 400 g good quality 00 flour type, plus extra for dusting.

Preparation:

It is royal pasta dough, velvety pasta, silk, made with a pure blend of fine semolina which has a golden color and a wonderful flavor, and 00 flour (00 means super fine.) This blend of free-range egg yolks along with flours gives you the ultimate in pasta dough. The best part of it is that it's super cheap based on the pasta volume it gives you. Roll or cut into hundreds of different shapes. Enjoy and feel the joy and pride of making pasta from scratch by yourself.

The pasta world is full of old wives' tales and rules of the dos and don'ts but throughout the whole of Italy, in every town, region or village, they frequently contradict each other. This particular method gets you in the right place but you can still roll out thicker to get a thicker noodle, which you will have to cook longer. The critical question to consider is this. Will it go well with the sauce you want to pair it with? The pasta shape and the sauce should be in harmony. The pasta equals to the sauce.

The dough

Pile the semolina and flour in a bowl and scoop a well at the center. Separate the eggs and pour in the yolks. For the egg whites, put them into a sandwich bag and put them in the freezer. Keep them to make meringues the next day.

To the well, add 4 tablespoons water and the oil and using a fork, whip up with the eggs until they are smooth and bring the flour gradually.

Clean your hands and flour them and get them in there and bring the dough together to form a ball when it becomes too hard to mix. Dust a work surface with flour and knead for about 4 minutes until elastic or smooth. Flour can differ in humidity and eggs differ in size. The dough should not be too dry or too wet. Add more flour or water if you desire. Cover with a cling film and allow about 30 minutes to rest.

Rolling out

Customarily, Italians used to have a giant rolling pin. If you like you also can do it in that way but it requires some elbow grease and a large flat surface. In this modern era, it's advisable and fun using a pasta machine. For a machine, firmly fix the machine to a clean and nice table and cut the pasta dough in four pieces and so that it does not dry out as you proceed. Cover it with a damp clean tea towel.

Stage 1

Flatten every piece of the pasta dough one at a time and run in on the thickest setting and take down the rollers by two parameters and then rerun the dough to get a thinner one. You can fold it into two and run it back again on the thickest setting. If you repeat this several times, it makes the dough very smooth and turns it into one that will fill the pasta machine out from a tatty sheet.

Stage 2

Roll the pasta sheet down on every setting and flour a little as you proceed. To avoid any ripples, folds or kinks, use one hand to turn the crank while maintaining a low tension with the other side. Take it down until you obtain the thickness you desire which is supposed to be 2 mm for shapes like tagliatelle, Lasagna and linguine. For tortellini and ravioli turned into filled pasta, go for a thinness of 1 mm because it doubles to 2 mm when folded around a filling.

Chestnut Pasta Dough

Ingredients:

- 200 g Whole wheat flour

- 400 g Chestnut flour

- 6 eggs

- 1 pinch of salt

- 200 g 00 flour

Equipment:

- Pasta maker

- Rack

- Rolling pin

Farina di Castagna is the Italian chestnut flour that we use to make this delicious recipe. This flour is very well ground and the ideal pasta flour. With a pasta maker, things are going to be quite easy for you.

For this pasta, you start by mixing chestnut flour and whole wheat flour and make a well at the center. Add eggs and salt and use your hands to mix. Knead to form dough that is soft and then cover and allow 30 minutes to rest.

Use a pasta maker to roll the dough as possibly thin and cut into shape of choice.

If you will not immediately cook the pasta, dust it with flour or semolina and place it on a rack to dry.

Buckwheat Pasta Dough

Ingredients:

- 125 ml water
- 2 egg whites
- 300 g Buckwheat flour

Equipment:

- Freezer
- Tray
- Table

STEP 1 - By hand

You can make this pasta dough using buckwheat and egg yolks. You start by mixing the flour and the egg yolks. Make a well in the middle and add water. For this dough you don't add salt. Use your hands to knead the dough, adding water if it is too dry. The dough should be smooth and shouldn't stick on your fingers.

Dust a table with flour and place the dough there.

STEP 2 - With Regina

Insert some dough in the Regina hopper. Turn the crank. After some time, the pasta comes out. When it gets to the length you want, use a slicer to cut.

Repeat the process for the remaining dough. Dust a tray or a cloth with flour and place the pasta there.

You can store the pasta in a freezer, and eat within a month.

Homemade Red Pasta Dough

Ingredients:

- 3 Large eggs

- 1 pinch of salt

- 2 ½ cups type 00 flour

- 1 tbsp. water

- ½ tbsp. tomato pastel

- 3 egg yolks

Equipment:

- Tray

- Bowl

- Plastic wrap

- Pasta machine/rolling pin

- Refrigerator

This pasta is made red by adding some tomato paste. You start by the flour to a tray or working surface and make a well in the middle. You then crack in the eggs, add tomato paste and salt and mix. Add in water little by little and knead using hands until dough is smooth and soft.

Form a ball and put it in bowl and use a plastic wrap to cover. To make it firm, put in a refrigerator for 30-60 minutes.

The next thing is to use the pasta machine to roll the dough into shape of choice. Alternatively, you can use a rolling pin.

Homemade Whole Wheat Pasta Dough

Ingredients:

- 200 g 00 flour

- 2 ¼ cups, white whole wheat flour

- 1 yolk

- 4 eggs

- ½ tsp. sea salt

Equipment:

- Rolling pin

- Pizza cutter/Knife

- Damp towel

- Electric crank

This recipe requires just three ingredients; white whole-wheat flour, eggs and salt. Just like with many pasta recipes, you start mixing the ingredients on a flat surface and making a well at the center. Crack in the eggs and add salt and mix. Knead with hands to form smooth and soft dough. When done, use a damp towel to cover and allow 30 minutes to rest.

Cut the dough into 8 pieces and use hands to flatten each of them and of course dusting each with flour. Roll the dough into thin sheets using a hand or electric crank. Unlike many other pasta doughs, in this one you proceed to make noodles using fettuccine attachment. You can also cut into strips of a quarter inch using a pizza cutter or a knife. Repeat until the dough is finished.

Tip:

You can use a rolling pin if you do not have an attachment to flatten the pasta into thin sheets.

Flour and Water Pasta Dough

Ingredients:

- 50 ml water

- 100 g All-purpose flour

Equipment:

- Fork

- Pasta machine

- Wooden gnocchi board

It is the most straightforward pasta dough to make. You simply mix the water and the flour and form dough. You add more water if it is too dry and little flour if it is too sticky.

On a flour-dusted surface, knead together and divide it into pieces. Mold them into the shapes you desire. For gnocchi, use hands and roll the piece's sausage-like parts of thickness of about 1.5 cm. Roll them on a wooden gnocchi board that ridges and if you do not have one, you can roll on a back of a fork.

Alternatively, you could use a pasta machine to roll them and make fettuccine or tagliolini. You can as well form strozzapreti by rolling small pieces on your palm.

Green Pasta Dough

Ingredients:

- 40 g Boiled, steamed and drained spinach

- 400 g All-purpose flour or 00 flour and more for rolling out

- 3 large eggs

- 2 pinches of salt

Equipment:

- Pasta machine/ Rolling pin

- Refrigerator

- Plastic wrap

- Stand mixer

The difference between this pasta and the others is that it is green in color. The green color is got from spinach. You start by blending cooked spinach and eggs for 10 minutes. Mix the salt, flour and spinach/egg mixture in a stand mixer until a ball is formed. Add flour is the dough is sticky or water a tablespoon at a time if it is dry. Do this until you get smooth and homogenous dough. Use a plastic wrap to cover it and refrigerate for half an hour.

Divide into four pieces and flatten them into rectangles and flour every part on every side. Put one piece into the pasta machine. Fold the ends inside and put it into the machine once again. Proceed with the remaining dough. By the way, you can use a rolling pin if you do not have a stand mixer but make sure that you flour the working surface well.

Dust a work surface with flour and place the pasta sheets there for about 10 minutes to dry. Fix the fettuccine accessory and put one layer through the machine. Proceed with the remaining pasta. Ensure that the fettuccine ribbons floured well, so avoid them sticking together. You can alternatively use hand in fettuccine to cut the pasta sheet.

Basic Orecchiette Pasta Dough

Ingredients:

- 11/2 cups, All-purpose flour, unbleached

- 1 cup semolina flour

- 2/3 cup, warm water

Equipment:

- Plastic wrap

- Rolling pin/Pasta machine

- Knife

- Dish towel

- Disk

- Jars

- Baking sheets

You can make this dough with sauce of uncooked basil and tomatoes, broccoli rabab sauce or ice cream sauce with mint and mussels. You start by mixing flours and making a well in the middle. Add water a teaspoon at a time as you stir with your hand. Continue until you get smooth and soft dough.

Dust a working surface with flour and kneed you get a supple and smooth result. Cut a piece of the dough the size of a golf ball and then use plastic wrap to cover the remaining dough. Roll to form a cylinder using a pasta machine or a rolling pin into a diameter of one inch. Slice the cylinder using a knife into 3mm thick disks.

Get a disk and press it on the palm of your hand and use the thumb of the other hand to press. Swivel your hand two times to make the center of the ear thinner and let the rim to be a bit thicker. Place it on a clean dishtowel. Repeat for the remaining dough. Once done, drizzle some flour on the ears and repeat until all dough is finished.

To store the pasta, spread the rounds on baking sheet with flour. Leave them overnight at room temperature. Once dry, store the orecchiette in covered jars at room temperature.

Pici Pasta Dough

Ingredients:

- 1 ¾ cups All-purpose flour

- 1 tbsp. olive oil

- 1 cup semolina flour

- 7/8 cup, water

- A pinch of salt

Equipment:

- Fork

- Plastic wrap

- Refrigerator

- Rolling pin/ Pasta machine

- Knife

For this recipe, you start by mixing salt and the flours and then making a well at the middle. Add oil and then water, a little by little. Use a fork to start forming dough. Switch to using your hand to mix the dough and then knead until it is smooth and soft. Use a plastic wrap to cover and let it rest for an hour, or you can alternatively refrigerate for up to one day.

Form the dough into a round shape and cut into four pieces. Use a plastic wrap to cover the pieces. Dust a working surface with flour to get it ready. Use your hand to flatten a piece of dough and dust with flour. Roll using a rolling pin and slice into quarter inch lengths.

To make pici, you roll the edges inwards in order to keep them moist. If your environment is dry, make sure that you cover with a plastic wrap or a cloth. Use a knife to cut a round piece and use a rolling pin to roll the pasta outwards from the middle to a diameter of ¼ inch. Make the pici as skinnier as possible.

A pici that is finished should be 8-inches long, You can also elongate them up to 18 inches. Do not make it any longer. Lay them on semolina or cornmeal-dusted pasta and use a cloth to cover when a sheet is complete.

Bigoli Pasta Dough

Ingredients:

- 3 eggs (You can as well use duck eggs)

- 400 g 00 flour or cake flour

- 1 tsp. salt

- 2 tbsp. water

Equipment:

- Cylinder

- Fork

You start by mixing eggs and flour using a fork until clumps are formed in the flour. Use hands to mix while adding water and flour where need be. Transfer to a flour-dusted working surface and knead the dough. Ensure that press is floured in the cylinder, as bigoli is customary prepared using it. Twist it and then cut two times for a dough load off one cylinder. You will have to use your flour sparingly so that the pasta does not stick. The dough should be hard and smooth.

Corzetti Pasta Dough

Ingredients:

- 200 g semolina flour

- 200 g plain flour

- Water or dry white wine

- 4 fresh eggs

- 1 pinch of salt

- 1 tsp. extra virgin olive oil

Equipment:

- Fork

- Wooden cutting board

- Rolling pin/Pasta machine

- Cutter

- Kitchen towel

- Knife

For this dough you start by combining the semolina flour and the plain flour in a wooden bowl or wooden cutting board. Form a well at the center and add eggs, salt and the extra-virgin olive oil.

Little by little, incorporate the flours and eggs using a fork until dough starts forming. Switch to using your hands and knead the dough till it does not stick and is elastic. Add flour if the dough is too wet and add water if it is too dry. Allow about 30-40 minutes to rest.

Use a rolling pin to roll the dough to a thickness of 1 mm. Use the cutter on the corzetti stamp or a knife and cut many rounds as you are able to. Place one round on the corzetti stamp and press the stamp edges using your hand to perfectly fit the pasta in. press the pasta disk using a handle of the corzetti stamp and turn on both directions.

Place the corzetti on a parchment or kitchen towel. Set them to dry if you are not cooking immediately.

Garganelli Pasta Dough Recipe

Ingredients:

- 4 eggs

- Pinch of salt

- 1 ½ cup semolina flour

- ½ cup All-purpose flour

- Extra flour for dusting

Equipment:

- Special pin/ Simple chopstick/ Round wooden pencil

- Rolling pin/Pasta machine

- Fridge

- Plastic wrap

- Fork

- Wooden table

Mix the flours on a wooden surface and make a well at the middle and add in salt and beaten eggs. Use a fork to incorporate the mixer until it is crumbly. If you do not mind, you can use your hands too.

Use your hands to knead until the dough is elastic, smooth and soft. Cover with a plastic wrap and allow about 15-35 minutes to rest. You can alternatively store overnight in a fridge.

Cut a piece of dough and use you hand to flatten it a bit. On a flour-dusted surface, roll the dough using a rolling pin. If you have a pasta machine, pass the dough on the widest setting and fold it into half before passing it again through the pasta machine on the same setting. Change the setting to about 1 mm thickness and put each piece into the machine. Dust a working surface with flour and set the ready sheet there.

Cut every sheet into a square of 1.5x1.5 inches and allow about 15-20 minutes to dry. This prevents garganelli from being flat when ready.

To shape the garganelli, you start by placing the pasta square on gnocchi board, which is floured. Fold a square corner over the pin off the garganelli. You can alternatively use a round wooden pencil or a simple chopstick if you do not have special pin.

Roll using the pin applying pressure so as to imprint ridges and seal the garganelli. Repeat the process until the squares are finished and eventually the remaining dough.

Garlic & Parsley Pasta Dough

Ingredients:

- 2 cups 00 flour

- 1 bunch, Fresh parsley

- 1 tsp. salt

- ½ cup, water

- 2 garlic cloves

- 4 eggs

- 40 g garlic puree

- 1 tsp. olive oil

Equipment:

- Rolling pin

This pasta dough is quite easy. You start by combining egg, flour, salt, olive oil, chopped parsley and garlic. Knead the mixture until you get smooth and soft dough. Allow about 15 minutes for the dough to rest for making your pasta.

Yellow Flour Pasta Dough

Ingredients:

- 150 g Corn flour
- 5 eggs
- 1 yolk
- 250 g 00 flour
- Salt

Equipment:

- Fork
- Plastic wrap

This dough appears yellow in color. You start by pouring the flour on a clean working surface and making a well at the middle. Crack in the egg and use a fork to incorporate slowly until it starts to be clumpy. Switch to using your hands and keep kneading until you the dough form up. Scrap and discard any dried bits of dough and put them away.

Dust a working surface with some flour and knead the dough until it is smooth, soft, and not sticky. Divide it into 9 pieces that are equal and use a plastic wrap to cover them. Store the while covered at room temperature until you are ready to prepare them. You can also form into shapes of choice if you desire.

Chapter 2: How to Prepare the Dough

There are two major types of pasta dough in Italy:

Simple Pasta With Eggs

This pasta dough includes eggs and to prepare it, get a wooden board and on it pour the flour. In the middle, make a well and add eggs and get a fork for using to mix them. Once the mixture begins getting thick, you can begin using your hand and vigorously knead using the palm of your hands. Do this until you get homogeneous and smooth dough. You can now shape your dough into your desired pasta shapes.

When making egg-based pasta, eggs play a fundamental role in your success rate:

- Use only fresh eggs, of the highest possible quality.

- Break the eggs into a separate bowl before adding them to the flour to make sure they are not spoiled.

- For best results, bring the eggs to room temperature before using them in your dough.

- When making egg pasta dough, always use large eggs with an average weight of about 2 ounces each.

Flour and Water Pasta Dough

Pasta dough with flour and water is one of the simplest to make. All you need to do is to mix the flour with the water and make dough. If the dough is too sticky, you can add a little flour and if it's too dry, you can add a little water.

Go on a surface that has been flour dusted and use your hands to knead. Knead continuously until you get smooth and elastic dough. Mold them in the pasta shapes you want.

Ingredients:

- 1 tablespoon olive oil

- 1 2/3 cups Italian 00 flour

- 2 large eggs

- Pinch sea salt

Preparation:

1. Put the flour on a clean pastry board and make a well at the middle using your fist.

2. In the well, break eggs and put them, also add oil and a pinch of salt. If you want to color your dough, at this point you can add the ingredients

3. Using a fork, mix the eggs into the flour until it becomes clumpy. Switch to using your hands to form a firm dough by bringing the ingredients together. Add some few drops of water if the dough is too dry and if too wet, add a little more flour. As time goes on you get used to how dough should feel after making it for several times. Note that your

pasta will taste floury and be tough if you add to much flour.

4. Knead the pasta dough for 2 to minutes until its smooth. Massage the dough lightly with olive oil. Use a resalable plastic bag and tuck the dough and leave it to rest at room temperature for at least 30 minutes. The dough will be more elastic than it was before after resting.

Passing the pasta dough through the pasta machine

1. You can choose to use a long wooden rolling pin to roll the dough into a pasta machine is better and makes the work less.

2. Set the machine on widest setting and feed the blob of pasta dough through the machine. When the pasta dough sheet comes out, fold it starting from the edges pass it into the rollers again on that widest setting. Pass it several times on the widest setting. This replaces kneading the dough and ensures the pasta is smooth and silky.

3. Repeatedly pass the dough sheet through the machine and reducing the setting slowly until you get the thickness you desire. If you unable to keep the dough from folding on

itself since the sheet of pasta dough tends to become long, you can cut the sheet of dough in halves and separately feed through every half.

4. When you get the desired thickness, hang it of the back of a chair or over a broom handle for it to dry a little. This makes cutting easier as it's not stick especially in humid weather. However, if you are in a hurry, you can use a little flour to dust the pasta and let it rest for just a short time on clean kitchen towels.

5. You can now shape the dough in your desired pasta

Fresh Egg Pasta (Puff Pastry and Shapes)

Prep time: 15 minutes

Serves: 4

Difficulty: Easy

Cost: Very low

Ingredients:

- 4 organic eggs

- 400 g 00 flour

Preparation:

1. To prepare fresh pasta, pour flour on a wooden pasta board or a bowl (a wooden board is preferred). Make a well at the middle and add in eggs and use a fork to mix them. When it starts becoming thick switch to using hands and knead vigorously with the palm of your hand until the dough becomes smooth.

2. Use a tablecloth or a cling film to cover the dough and allow a minimum of 30 minutes at room temperature to rest.

3. Use a tarot to cut a piece of the dough and leave the rest covered. Flour the piece and use a dough sheeter to pull it

to the maximum thickness. Get the dough and pass between rollers to form thick dough.

4. Fold from the edges towards the middle and drizzle with some little flour. Pass it between rollers again until a rectangular sheet is formed. Flour a surface and lay the sheet there and use a knife or a tarot to trim the edges. Divide the sheet into two, occasionally passing the thinnest to the thickest. Your pasta is ready.

STORAGE

You store the pasta in a freezer in shape of choice in a tray for a few hours for them to harden. When hard, transfer them to frost bags and return them to the freezer. To use you start by adding them to boiling water and continue as per instructions.

TIPS FOR GREAT FRESH PASTA!

1. It is better using a pastry board because the wooden surface is rough which is better than a surface that is smooth.

2. Use a fork to beat the eggs into the well to avoid them coming out.

3. You can add a pinch of salt if you desire.

4. Do not use currents as it makes the pasta dry.

5. Egg-flour ratio should be one egg to 100 g of flour.

6. Processing: you must take a minimum of 10 minutes to process the dough, using the palm of your hand and occasionally beat on the board to improve its elasticity.

7. Always ensure that the dough that is not being worked on is covered to avoid it drying.

8. Dust the work surface to prevent the pasta from sticking to the working surface.

9. It is advisable to dry the semolina drizzled spreadsheets on every side some minutes before you fold them to roll that is flat in case you need to make quadrucci, pappardelle, tagliolini, tagliatelle or lasagna.

10. Yolks or eggs? You can unbalance them when making stuffed pasta like tortellini or ravioli. For 140g flour, add yolk+ egg. For dry pasta, use a whole egg only.

How to Prepare Fresh Homemade Pasta

Fresh homemade is not just food! It has become a way of life both in Italy and in the rest of the world. It has been passed from one generation to another in people's families; it is a moment of happiness and celebration with friends and family. The fresh pasta is an Italian tradition that has been there for decades.

 Making fresh pasta takes patience, attention and time; to get that pasta with pleasant roughness, right consistency and cooking it right.

Macaroni, orecchiette, ravioli, lasagna or tagliatelle are way much tastier when homemade. They are also easy to prepare. You just need some few ingredients that are also easily available at the stores.

The exact place of origin of pasta is not known because there have been many places that have been alleged to be the origin of pasta. There is an assumption that the pasta discovery was a slow process. From a mix of water and crushed wheat to the discovery of bread and pasta. The fresh pasta originated from the Mediterranean and Asia.

The making of fresh homemade pasta in Italy varies from South to North. In Southern and Central Italy, the dough is prepared using water and durum wheat semolina which has been re-milled; trofie, bucatini, cavatelli, orecchiette, macaroni are examples. In the northern part, the homemade pasta is usually soft and made with eggs and flour. Stuffed pasta, pici, bigoli, cannelloni, garganelli and lasagna are examples.

Any dough type chosen makes a variety of shapes. as soon as you have rolled your pasta out and cut it into shape of choice, you can cook right away.

Add some extra virgin olive oil to the water when cooking to ensure that the fresh pasta does not stick as you cook. It is also advisable not to use a colander when draining, but instead use a perforated ladle. The final result can be spoiled by colander.

There are several sauces with which you can serve the pasta with. They include meat, Mediterranean dressing vegetables, fish and many more.

How to prepare the dough for fresh homemade pasta?

Traditionally, the dough that has been used to make egg pasta. The ingredients quantities vary depending on the pasta type you want to prepare. With the recipe below, you are going to know how to make egg dough that is perfect:

Ingredients:

- 4 eggs

- 400g flour 00

- Salt

Preparation:

1. Start by pouring the flour on a pastry board and form a well at the middle. Add salt and break in the egg into the well.

2. Use a fork and start incorporating the mixture starting from the edges nearby until it starts to be clumpy.

3. Switch to using your fingers and ensure that you have incorporated all the flour into the eggs.

4. When the dough starts becoming consistent, use your hands, pulling it in all directions back and forth. Lift it off the pastry board and scrape off any bits of dough stuck on the sides using a spatula and knead it.

5. After vigorously kneading for about 10 minutes, form a ball and use a plastic wrap to cover it. Let the dough rest for about 30 minutes.

6. Cut a small piece of the dough and use your hands to flatten it into a disk. Dust the work surface with flour and place the disc on top. Use a rolling pin, moving it in every direction, to make it into the thickness you desire.

   If you have a pasta machine, pass the disk on the rolls. Fold it into 2 layers and pass it through the rollers to thin it. You can repeat the process in order to get regular shape and the thickness you desire.

7. To form tagliolini and tagliatelle or other classic cuts, roll the sheet from the edges.

8. Cut the dough using a sharp knife into 3mm thick strips for the tagliolini and 1cm thick strips for the tagliatelle. You can alternatively use a machine and cut the dough into the format you want.

9. Your pasta is now ready and you cook immediately if you desire or store.

Tips

1. To make water and flour pasta, you use the same procedure as the one above; however, in the well at the middle of the flour, add lukewarm water and a pinch of salt. The water:

flour ratio should be 1:2. Using durum wheat semolina other than flour results to a cook-resistant pasta. You can get pastas like trofie, bucatini, cavatelli, corzetti, orecchiette etc. using this dough type. All these have a sustained thickness and should not be left so much al dente when you cook them.

2. To make the green pasta, you use the same preparation steps for egg and flour pasta dough. What you need to pay attention to most is the ingredients doses: decrease the water and egg quantity as vegetables have water in them; furthermore, it is advisable using very few egg yolks to ensure the green color is retained by the pasta.

Chapter 3: The Most Important Tools Used to Make the Dough

The Art of Italian Fresh Pasta

This art of making the homemade pasta is very crucial in the Italian tradition. Even though the fresh pasta recipes always vary from one region to another for example the type of flour, water, eggs, salt and olive oil, all are elements that may be there or not even there and are also in various quantities. The common thing in this practice of ancient times that was born in families that used simple ingredients and tools.

In the modern world, this tradition is practiced less in the families as many Italian women work more form outside the home. Good enough this practice is still alive in the grand mothers and is mostly applied by companies, restaurants and specialized schools.

Who is known as a puff pastry? This is a person who makes handmade pasta traditionally using a rolling pin and a wooden board. This is a traditional name. It used to be an informative and fun way. The tools below are great and aid in making perfect homemade fresh pasta.

Essential Tools

These are the tools that you really can't make pasta without. But don't panic! Most of these are items you already own.

Pasta Machine

This is a very useful piece of equipment to have, especially if you are planning to make pasta often or for more than two people. It saves you a lot of time and effort, as it does the rolling for you, and it also ensures a uniform thickness to the pasta sheets. You can get a manual machine or a motorized one. I have a manual one and I love it, but the choice is yours. Pasta machines often come with attachments to cut pasta ribbons, like tagliatelle and/or tagliolini, which are very useful too.

Baking Sheets

You need three baking sheets (10 by 15 inches in size) on which to place your ready pasta before cooking it. Make sure to always dust the baking sheets with a couple of tablespoons of flour so that the pasta doesn't stick to the surface.

Big Wooden Board

You need a big wooden board or at least a big wooden cutting board to give pasta like orecchiette and strascinati their characteristic rough surface to which the sauce clings.

Rolling Pin

Using a rolling pin to roll out pasta both non-egg and egg is very relaxing. A long, thin, European-style rolling pin is useful when making pasta that requires rolling out, like ribbon pasta, for example. It is essential if you do not have a pasta machine.

Cookie/Pasta Cutters

Cookie cutters can be very useful when making stuffed pasta. You need a heart-shaped cookie cutter to make hearts and a star-shaped cookie cutter to make stars. You also need round pasta/cookie cutters to make different shapes of stuffed pasta. You will need one each of 1½-inch, 2½-inch, 3-inch, and 5-inch diameters. Alternatively, you can use a glass or a bowl of the same diameter as a guide and a no serrated knife to cut around it.

Kitchen Scale

Making pasta from scratch is very easy when you have the right dough, and to obtain the right dough, the best thing to do is to precisely weigh the ingredients. This is particularly important when you are just starting out and are not yet familiar with the correct look and feel of good pasta. A weighing scale is a really important tool when it comes to pasta making, and I highly recommend you use one.

Knives

You need a good, sharp, no serrated cutting knife to cut out your dough and turn it into pasta or gnocchi. You'll use a round-edged table knife to give pasta like orecchiette and corzetti its typical shape.

Crinkle-Edge Pastry Wheel and/or Pizza Cutter

You need a crinkle-edge pastry wheel to make stuffed pasta, like ravioli or caramelle, look prettier, and you also need it to give ribbon pasta, like mafalde and rombi, its characteristic shape. In some cases, a pizza cutter can be used instead of a crinkle-edge pastry wheel or a knife. You can cut out more pasta in less time if you use one.

Knitting Needle

You need a knitting needle size 0 or 1 to make pasta like maccheroni al ferretto, fusilli avellinesi, or busiati.

Metal Cake Spatula

You need a round-edged metal cake spatula to give pasta like Strascinati its typical shape. It serves the same purpose as a table knife, but it is much bigger and better suited for broader shapes of pasta. You can use it instead of the specific tool to make Strascinati, which is very hard to find.

Plastic Wrap

Plastic wrap is essential to keep your dough from drying out. Make sure to always wrap the dough tightly with plastic wrap before leaving it to rest. You should also use it to cover the dough whenever you are not working on it. If the dough dries out, it will create a crust and start breaking, and it will not be possible to shape it anymore.

Potato Ricer

A potato ricer is very useful for making gnocchi. It processes the potatoes (and other vegetables) by forcing them through a sheet of small holes, giving a smoother texture to the mash, which in turn gives you much smoother and more uniform gnocchi dough.

Non-Essential Tools

The following tools are nice to have and come in handy for making specialty pasta shapes, but they are by no means necessary.

Big Bowl

You may use a bowl to bring together all your dough ingredients before transferring it onto your work surface to knead it.

Dough Scraper

A dough scraper is a tool used to manipulate dough and to clean the surfaces on which the dough has been worked. It is generally a small sheet of stainless steel (approximately 3 by 5 inches) with a handle of wood or plastic. It can be very useful when making pasta dough, but it's not essential.

Gnocchi Board

A gnocchi board is a small wooden board with ridges that give gnocchi their traditional shape. If you can find it, the one that comes with the mini rolling pin is also perfect for making garganelli. This tool is inexpensive and a great gadget to have, but it is not essential. If you don't have one, you can use a fork to give gnocchi their typical ridges.

Food Processor

If you have a food processor, you can use it to blend all the ingredients to bring the dough together until the flour looks like coarse breadcrumbs. Then you can transfer the mixture onto the work surface and knead it.

Pasta Frame and Drying Rack

A pasta frame is a wooden frame fitted with a thin mesh. It's used to keep short pasta to dry. A drying rack is used to hang long pasta to dry.

Stand Mixer

If you have a stand mixer, you can use it to make your dough. You will need both paddle and hook attachments to bring the dough together and knead it.

Dry Pasta Stand

This dryer is exclusively designed for long fresh pasta shapes. You can be able to hang your tagliolini, pappardelle, spaghetti and tagliatelle on the guitar. When you hang them there, they dry well and won't stick to each other and will be perfect when the cooking time comes.

Chapter 4: Long Pasta Recipes

Scialatielli

Prep time: 15 minutes

Serves: 6

Difficulty: Very Easy

Cost: Very low

Ingredients:

- 1 egg

- 175 g whole milk

- Basil

- 10 g, extra virgin olive oil

- 30 g grated pecorino

- 400 g durum wheat semolina

Preparation:

How to prepare the scialatielli

1. Wash and dry the basil leaves and chop them finely with a knife. Pour the durum wheat in the bowl and add the beaten egg with the use of a fork.

2. Add the chopped basil, the grated pecorino and flush at room temperature after adding the milk.

3. Pour in the extra virgin olive oil and start kneading using the hand.

4. After transferring the mixture onto the pastry board, continue kneading again by hand for like 8 minutes.

5. Get homogeneous and smooth dough; leave it to rest for about 30 minutes at room temperature after wrapping it in a cling film.

6. Divide the dough into two 10s, and keep the other half, wrap it in a plastic wrap so as to prevent it from drying out because of the air. On the pastry board, work on the first part flour it with semolina using a rolling pin of about 5 mm thick.

7. After sprinkling the pastry with more semolina, drag the edges towards the center by rolling them form one side to the other till you reach the center.

8. Cut the dough into rings about 1 cm thick using a well-sharpened blade. With the help of your hands, unroll them gently. They must be like 12-15 cm long.

9. At such a point, your scialatielli are ready to be cooked in plentiful boiling and salted water for like 5 minutes.

STORAGE

You can prepare the scialatielli and allow them to dry by air for few minutes. Keep them on a try with a cloth that is floured with semolina.

You may as well freeze the dough. In such a case, pull and cut the dough to get nests that you will put on a tray with the dish towel. Put them in the frost bags for food once they are frozen.

ADVICE

How can you season this institution of Campania cuisine? With seafood cooked together in a pan with some cherry tomatoes for taste enhancement. You can as well try a vegetarian and white version like with sautéed courgettes.

Tagliolini Fatti in Casa (Homemade Tagliolini)

Prep time: 30 minutes

Cook time: 5 minutes

Serves: 4

Difficulty: Easy

Cost: Very low

Ingredients:

For fresh pasta:

- 2 medium eggs

- Semolina for pastry board

- 200 g 00 flour

Preparation:

1. Pour the flour in a bowl, add eggs and mix with a fork. Use your hands to mix until you create a homogeneous mixture.

2. Take the dough to a work surface that is lightly floured and continue working vigorously.

3. If necessary, add a little flour and work until the dough is elastic and smooth.

4. Make a ball and wrap it in a plastic wrap or put it in a food bag in a dry and cool place at room temperature for like 30 minutes.

5. When the rest time is over. Take the pasta sprinkled with little flour and divide in two parts. To avoid drying, close the film you aren't using immediately. You can pull the other using the machine or rolling pin from the lowest to the highest till you acquire a very thin sheet.

6. Put the obtained strips on a work surface, lightly floured with refilled semolina, which you can as well use to sprinkle the pasta sheets. From each sheet, make 3 rectangles and let each side dry for like 3 minutes. Without pressing, wrap the rectangles on themselves to form small rolls and use a knife to cut them into 2 mm thick strips.

7. Taking a piece of pasta, unroll the tagliolini delicately. Roll into a nest and let them dry on a clothesline or a lightly and clean floured dish towel. Continue that process till you finish all the fresh pasta.

STORAGE

It is usually better to immediately consume the tagliolini or else it can be kept for a day in the refrigerator.

You can freeze the tagliolini raw. On a tray, put the well-spaced nests of pasta and put them in a freezer for some hours so that they can harden. Put them in frost bags once they harden and place them back in the freezer. Once you want to use them, directly boil them in boiling water from frozen.

Pappardelle Fatte in Casa (Homemade Pappardelle)

Prep time: 30 minutes

Cook time: 10 minutes

Serves: 3

Difficulty: Low

Cost: Low

Ingredients:

- 3 eggs

- 300 g 00 flour

Preparation:

1. To prepare the homemade pappardelle, put the flour in a bowl or on the work surface. Break the eggs and lightly beat them using a fork.

2. Add flour to the eggs until they have absorbed the flour and on a work surface or table, start kneading using the hand. Use the palms pf your hands to work until you obtain a smooth and homogenous mixture.

3. This operation takes quite some time. To prove that all is in the right place, cut it into halves and when you see air bubbles, just know you have done a great job.

4. Make a loaf and put in closed in a plastic wrap and allow it to rest on your work surface for 15-20 minutes

5. Slightly flour the surface use a rolling pin to roll out the dough beginning from the center. Use the rolling pin to roll the dough, roll as you lightly press on the upper right and left edges. Again, roll them out and continue the same operation until you get the thickness you desire. Allow it to dry for 10 minutes.

6. Use a little flour to sprinkle the dough and slightly fold the edges at the top and bottom, roll until it reaches at the center of the pasta circle and do it on both sides. Use a sharp knife to cut the strips 1 cm wide and unroll the strips.

7. Use the palm of your hand to roll the pappardelle a little at a time and put them on a lightly floured tray after forming a nest.

8. Cook and season them as preferred.

Lasagne

Prep time: 20 minutes

Serves: 6

Difficulty: 2

Ingredients:

- 4 eggs

- 1 pinch of salt

- 400 g 00 flour

Preparation:

1. Clean the work surface and make sure it is uncluttered and smooth.

2. In a classic fountain shape, pour in the flour and after you make a hole in the center, pour the shelled eggs inside and also add a pinch of salt. Use a fork to beat the eggs slowly and then move on to the more certainly and traditional method of using the fingers.

3. Incorporate the flour gradually on the edges until all ingredients are well mixed. When you get your egg pasta

ball, start working on it by occasionally beating it on the lightly floured pastry board and also vigorously massaging it. This phase should last for at least 15 minutes to 1 hour. Use a damp cloth to wrap the dough and allow it to rest for 30 minutes.

4. On a floured surface, take the dough again and massage it a little more. Begin pressing it with your hands as you roll it then to form a very thin sheet use the rolling pin, make a sheet less than a millimeter.

5. You can as well divide the dough into several portions that will be rolled out one at a given time. This will facilitate and ease this operation.

6. Depending on the size of the pan, you can now cut the pasta in rectangles of variable sizes or the shape of Lasagna. (The formats used most are 8x16 cm or 14x20)

7. You can now think about how to season the different layers after the sheet is ready.

ADVICE

You should massage and work on the dough for a long time in order to get elastic and smooth dough.

Try and avoid working from an environment, which is categorized with cold drafts.

Always add few tablespoons of warm water if you realize that the pasta excessively dries out.

Add 200 g of whisked, cooked and squeezed spinach to get green Lasagna.

Pici Fatti a Mano (Handmade Pici)

Prep time: 1 hour

Cook time: 10 minutes

Serves: 4

Difficulty: Medium

Cost: Very cheap

Ingredients:

- 270 ml warm water

- 2 tbsp olive oil

- 1 pinch of salt

- 450 g 00 flour

Preparation:

Hand-making

On a pastry board, use 450 g of flour and make a fountain. Pour about 270 ml and lukewarm water and also add salt. Add a tablespoon of oil and begin kneading. Use your hands to knead for a long time till you get a smooth, very firm and homogeneous dough. You can add small amounts of flour and water if necessary.

In planetary

In a bowl, add oil, salt and water, run at speed 2 and then add the flour, spoon after spoon until you obtain a paste that is consistent. When the pasta twists around the hook without almost or even adhering to it, just know it's ready. Start by using the spatula then the kneading hook.

How they are made (appiciatura)

1. Make the dough into a ball and put it in a plastic wrap. Let it rest for like 30 minutes after covering it with cloth. Knead it for like half a minute and take it back. On a floured surface, use a rolling pin to roll it to the thickness of 1 inch or even less. Use few oil drops to grease it and cut it into strips as large as they are high in a less or more square section.

2. Sprinkle a little wheat flour on the pastry board. Use a couple of handfuls of yellow or corn flour to prepare the tray and as you make the pici, it will help to dry them.

3. Use the fingers of your left hand to take the end of a strip and keep it raised slightly from the pastry board. Use the

palm of your right hand and roll it over by rubbing and use the left hand to stretch it by pulling gently. This will enable you get a long spaghetti which you will make of fairly and uniform fine diameter.

4. When done, for it to dry, throw it on the yellow surface and move it so that it sticks. You can repeat this for all the pasta. Make sure before you throw the pici in the tray, it has been well floured to avoid them from attacking each other. After you are done making all the pici, pass them on the pastry board. This should be after removing from the tray. Spread them out and separate them from each other but always flower them well with yellow flour.

5. Allow them to dry for at least 45 minutes and a maximum of 3 hours because when fully dry, they cook well. To avoid them touching the pastry board on the same side, move them occasionally. There is no problem in case they break while you move them, just attach together the ends that have broken and continue. Do not make them very long for the first few times. Two or three palms are okay.

Cooking

Use plenty of salted water to boil them for about 8 minutes. To avoid them sticking together, it's advisable to add a spoonful of oil in the cooking water. Gently take them and untie any agglomerates or knots that may have made them before cooking them. Throw them in boiling water in handfuls after freeing them from any excess flour.

ADVICE

For kneading, do not use hot or cold water. Use warm water. Use a large stove and boil them in much water because usually when they are thrown, they tend to lower the water temperature. When you boil them on a small stove or using little water, they will be sticky and will also take a long time to boil.

Once you remove them al dente, toss them in the pan with the sauce hot already, sauté or turn very little. Avoid adding cooking water so that they don't become sticky. The flour or the water or both should be measured when you make them. For each person, the dose that is normal is 1bout 65 g of water and 110 g of flour.

Not all flours absorb equally, so there could be small variations in the latter. To the initial dough, add an egg in the Montepulciano area using at least half a kilo of flour. With this, you get a more resistant and firmer paste.

Pasta Verde agli Spinaci (Green Pasta with Spinach)

Prep time: 60 minutes

Cook time: 10 minutes

Serves: 4

Difficulty: Medium

Cost: Low

Ingredients:

- 300 g 00 flour

- 3 medium eggs

- 60 g spinach

Preparation:

1. In making the green pasta with spinach, in a pan, put to boil 60 g of washed and drained spinach. Add a pinch of salt and water. Cover and allow them to cook and let the spinach dry and then pass it through a sieve to get a cream that is smooth.

2. Pour the sifter flour, the eggs that have been kept at room temperature and the spinach cream in a bowl and mix all the ingredients well.

3. Move to the pastry board and knead with your hands until you get homogeneous dough. If the dough is slightly hard or doesn't collect the flour completely, add 1 or 2 tablespoons of lukewarm water and keep kneading until the dough is compact and smooth and let it rests in a cool place covered for at least 30 minutes. Once the rest is done, the fresh pasta will be more elastic and softer. You can now prepare to roll it out and get the format you desire. You can use a machine or use the hands.

STORAGE

At the moment, we recommend using fresh egg pasta. If you want, you can keep it packed in vacuum for at most a couple of days.

Alternatively, once desired formats have you been made, it can be frozen raw.

Tagliatelle (Noodles)

Prep time: 30 minutes

Serves: 4

Difficulty: Medium

Ingredients

- 3 eggs at room temperature

- 300 g 00 flour

- Semolina to sprinkle

Preparation:

1. To prepare noodles, in a bowl, pour in the flour, make sure you remain with a little flour to add when necessary.

2. Create a basin and then break the eggs at room temperature in the center. Use a fork to beat the eggs and once they have absorbed some flour, keep kneading with a hand until you obtain a homogeneous mixture. On a lightly floured surface, keep kneading the dough for about 15 minutes until an elastic and smooth consistency is got.

3. Handle the glutinic mesh with energy but make sure you don't tear it. Make a ball and wrap it in a plastic wrap. Allow the dough to rest for 30 minutes at room temperature.

4. Divide the dough in 3 parts and then spread it easily. Flatten each part carefully after flouring it and keep other two parts in the film to avoid drying out.

5. Put the pasta machine on thickness mode for example maximum thickness and to obtain a first thick sheet, pass the dough through the rollers and to give a shape that is more regular, fold the two edges of the sheet towards the center and pass it between rollers again after flouring it lightly. Repeat this way until you get to the thickness you want.

6. Use a knife or tarot to level the dough obtained. This can be done on a floured pastry board to make the dough regular and in order to handle it easily, divide it into two parts. Using a thick machine, go over it again because you will have retired while working with it. Use a little semolina to sprinkle on both sides and leave the sheets to dry on each side for 5 minutes.

7. Fold a flap up to two thirds and take the sheet and begin rolling and create a flat roll. Cut the dough roll into slices of 7 mm thick while keeping the closure upwards.

8. From the ends, take the noodles on the hand and roll them around fingers in order to create a nest and let it to lay on a pastry board that is lightly floured. Continue the process until all the dough is finished. Now the noodles are ready, what remains is to cook them.

STORAGE

Raw noodles can be fee zed. To do so, on a tray, put the well-spaced nests of pasta and keep them in the freezer to harden for few hours. Once they harden, put them in frost bags and put them back in a freezer. Boil them directly from frozen in boiling water when you want to use them and then proceed per the recipe.

ADVICE

You can use a long rolling pin to roll out the fresh pasta if you prefer the traditional method. This will however take a lot of elbow grease and patience.

Fettuccine Fatte in Casa Ricetta della Nonna (Homemade Fettuccine Grandma's Recipe)

Prep time: 10 minutes

Serves: 5

Ingredients:

- 500 g 00 flour

- 5 whole eggs

- Salt

Preparation:

1. On a wooden worktop, arrange and make a classic fountain of flour by using your fingers to spread the central hole well. On a plate, break the eggs one by one and pour them in the fountain center and add a pinch of salt. It's advisable opt to break the eggs in the fountain directly. This is because you can run into a bad egg (This can be identified by the bad smells it gives once you have opened it. It is always recommended when making the dough with eggs;

break the eggs apart to avoid throwing away everything in case you find some eggs are spoilt.

2. When you have finished pouring the eggs in the fountain and seasoning them with salt, use a fork to gently beat them and add flour as you beat the eggs. This helps because it doesn't let the egg to run down for all sides. Another way that could be faster, use your hands to collect all the flour. Begin working with the mixture while kneading in order to get dry, smooth and not too soft dough.

3. Wrap the dough in a plastic wrap and allow it to rest for about 30 minutes. Meanwhile, start preparing the dressing for your homemade fettuccine.

4. Take the dough again after 30 minutes and on a wooden board, sprinkle a little flour. Use your hands to crust the dough a little to make a round pizza then use a rolling pin to begin rolling out. Cut the dough into two and make two sheets if you find it more comfortable to work using less dough.

5. As you use the rolling pin to roll out the dough while pulling and rubbing your palms on it, bringing them closer and also moving them away, put it on the table. Keep using the rolling pin to pull it and roll it up and also continue

rubbing with your hands until you obtain a sheet of about 1 or 2 millimeters.

6. When you get the desired sheet, spread it on the table and allow it dry for few minutes. Sprinkle with little flour and begin rolling up. Begin cutting the sheet into the sizes you want, using a sharp knife. From 5 to 6 millimeters for pappardelle and from 3 to 4 millimeters for tagliatelle and fettuccine.

7. Spread a large tablecloth or dishcloth once sliced, use your hands to spread the rolls and to unroll the fettuccine and arrange them, sprinkling a little flour on the dishcloth. Put a pan of water to boil to cook them while they are covered with a table or dish cloth.

8. Pour the fettuccine in the water once it boils and cook for 6 minutes. Serve and enjoy your meal.

Chapter 5: Short Pasta Recipes

Orecchiette

Prep time: 60 minutes

Serves: 6

Difficulty: Medium

Cost: Very low

Ingredients:

- 400 g durum wheat semolina

- 200 g lukewarm water

- ¼ tsp. salt

Preparation:

1. Pour the wheat flour on a pastry board

2. Create a fountain

3. Season with salt

4. Pour water at the middle and incorporate the flour using your fingers. Do a little at a time the water to be absorbed by the flour.

5. Use your hands to knead to form an elastic and homogeneous consistency. This takes approximately 10 minutes. Shape the dough into a circular shape and use a cloth to cover it. Rest for 15-20 minutes at room temperature.

6. After resting, cut a piece using a pastry cutter and leave the rest covered. Make a loaf whose thickness is about 1 cm. From the loaf, form smaller 1 cm pieces.

7. Use a blade knife that is smooth to form small shells on every piece. This is done by dragging the pieces on the pastry board, which is lightly floured towards you. Form the orecchiette by turning over the shell on itself. Repeat the process until the dough is finished and by the end you will have your Apulian orecchiette.

STORAGE

Use a cloth to dry the covered orecchiette. Store for about four weeks.

You can as well freeze them on a tray and when stiff, move to frost bags.

ADVICE

When cooking the orecchiette, do so in salted boiling water for 6 minutes. Use turnip greens to season them. You can also use a tomato sauce!

Farfalle

Prep time: 40 minutes

Cook time: 5 minutes

Serves: 4

Difficulty: Difficult

Cost: Low

Ingredients:

- 200 g 00 flour

- 2 medium Eggs

Preparation:

1. For the butterflies, you begin by putting the flour on a weighing scale, keep on adding it on the pastry board (leave some flour behind to add just in case the dough is too soft). Form a bowl at the middle and add the eggs. Start with a fork to mix, and then proceed using your hand. Knead until the dough is elastic and smooth consistently.

2. Form the dough into a sphere and cover it using a transparent film. Allow a minimum of 20 minutes for the pasta to rest.

3. After 20 minutes, divide the dough into quarters. Get one piece and place it in the pasta machine (leave the rest covered in a plastic wrap). Work on the dough until it is 1 mm thick.

4. Use a pastry cutter and make rectangular shapes on the sheets you got and with the notched part, form vertical strips with a width of 7 cm. With the smooth part, cut horizontally into 4 cm. Use your forefinger and thumb and to form butterflies. Lift a piece of dough at the rectangle's center using your thumb. You will create another fold at the middle; bring the other flap to the center using your index finger creating another fold.

5. Tighten the middle to fix the butterflies' shape; repeat for the remaining dough and put them on a tray.

6. While making the butterflies, lightly flour a tray and arrange them. Allow about 30 minutes to dry. Cook the butterflies in boiling water that is salted.

STORAGE

Put the dry pasta farfalle in frost bags and put in a freezer up to a month.

ADVICE

Use fresh spinach pasta to get green farfalle!

Cavatelli

Prep time: 15 minutes

Cook time: 10 minutes

Serves: 4

Difficulty: Difficult

Cost: Very Low

Ingredients:

- 125 g Durum wheat semolina

- 125 g 00 flour

- 130 g Water

- 1 tbsp Extra virgin olive oil

Preparation:

1. Mix the Durum wheat semolina and 00 flour in a bowl and move them to a pastry board to form a fountain at the middle. Mix by adding little water.

2. Add oil and keep on kneading to get soft and smooth dough and make it round.

3. Cover the pasta using a film and allow about 13 minutes to rest (this makes the dough elastic). Take a piece of pasta and form a tube. Divide it into pieces with a width of 1 cm.

4. To form the cavatelli, dig inside using some little pressure and curl the edges. Put it on a tray and drizzle the semolina over. Allow 2 hours for cavatelli to dry for it to be consistent when you cook (you can also cook immediately but it is advised against).

5. Add to salted boiling water and cook for about 8-10 minutes while constantly checking.

STORAGE

Refrigerate the cavatelli for up to 4 days. You can freeze the cavatelli for 30 minutes to avoid them sticking together.

You can store the dry cavatelli for up to 2 weeks.

ADVICE

More cooking time is needed as pasta dries. Therefore, you need to taste the cavatelli to check the cooking.

Strozzapreti Emiliani Fatti in Casa

(Homemade Emilian Strozzapreti)

Prep time: 30 minutes

Cook time: 5 minutes

Serves: 4

Difficulty: Medium

Cost: Low

Ingredients:

- 500 ml water

- 1 kg 00 flour

- ½ tsp. Salt

Preparation:

1. Mix 00 flour with salt and add water little by little as you mix with your hand. Keep kneading to until thoroughly mixed.

2. Move the dough to a working surface and knead to form homogeneous and smooth dough. Use a plastic wrap to cover and allow 30 minutes to rest.

3. In the meantime, cut the dough into two and leave one part covered. Roll the dough to about 1 mm thickness. Use a toothless blade knife to cut, and then use the tip of the knife to remove the strips to avoid sticking.

4. Use a cutter to cut 2 cm strips. For every strip, roll it starting from one end to form clams of at least 3 cm. Repeat the process until dough is finished.

5. Put the Strozzapreti trays that are floured lightly and keep it in the freezer until you are ready to use it.

Strascinati Fatti in Casa (Homemade Strascinati)

Prep time: 30 minutes

Serves: 4

Difficulty: Easy

Cost: Low

Ingredients:

- 200 ml water

- Salt

- 400 g durum wheat flour

Preparation:

1. Knead the mentioned ingredients until you get a hard and homogeneous mixture. If you want, you can use a machine for this process and then remove the mixture from the basket immediately you finish the mixing phase.

2. Use the mixture to make a ball and wrap it in a plastic wrap. Allow it to rest for 30 minutes. Divide the dough in many parts and using a lightly floured surface, work on every part

of the dough and make a long stick that has a diameter of 8 mm and cut them into pieces. This cut can be made approximately every 4-5 cm.

3. Press each piece of the dough and make the movement from top to the bottom using the three central fingers. Work on all the pasta that is available in this way and take care not to move the Strascinati that has been worked on, on a slightly and lightly floured spaced self to avoid them sticking together.

4. Allow them to dry for 30 minutes. After this, it's now possible to cook your homemade Strascinati.

Gnocchi di Patate (Potato Gnocchi)

Prep time: 20 minutes

Cook time: 40 minutes

Serves: 4

Difficulty: Easy

Cost: Very low

Ingredients:

- 1 medium egg

- 300 g 00 flour

- 1 kg potatoes

- Salt to taste

For the version without eggs:

- 350 g 00 flour

- 15 g salt

- 1 kg potatoes

Preparation:

1. In preparing this recipe, begin by pouring the flour on a pastry board and the boiling the potatoes. In a large pot, put the potatoes and cover them with much cold water.

2. When the water is boiling, depending on their size, count like 35 minutes. Use a fork to test. When the prongs enter the middle with little effort, know they are ready and drain them.

3. While still hot, peel and crush them immediately on the flour and then add the beaten egg and salt together and use your hands to mix them till you get compact but soft dough.

4. Don't forget that if you work on them a lot, the gnocchi will be hard while cooking and only knead the dough. Use your fingertips to roll out a piece of the dough to get the bigoli; the loves 2cm thick and for this, you should occasionally use semolina flour to dust the pastry board. To prevent the remaining dough from drying out, cover it with a tea towel.

5. Cut the loaves into chunks and to get a classic shape, drag on the gnocchi row by using your thumb to lightly press them. A fork can be used to drag them on prongs if you do

not have the gnocchi row and to avoid sticking, use semolina flour.

6. Lightly flour a dish towel and set it on a tray. Arrange the gnocchi on a tray, keeping space from one to the other.

7. To cook them, bring salted water to boil and pour them in and cook until they come to the surface. Season and drain and then serve.

For the version without eggs

1. While the potatoes are still hot, mash them on the pastry board using a potato masher. Add flour and salt and then use your hands to knead in order to get a compact but soft mixture.

2. Pick up a dough portion at a time and roll it using the tips of the fingers in order to form the loaves of 2 cm thickness. Cut the loaves in 5 pieces and pass every dough piece on the prongs of a fork or on a gnocchi row with the use of the thumb to lightly press.

3. Cook the dumplings eggless in much boiling salted water and as soon as they come to the surface, drain them.

STORAGE

You can keep the potato gnocchi raw by leaving it for a couple of hours on the cloth. But since they will have dried in the air, the cooking might be a bit longer.

Dumplings can also be freezing. For this, put the tray in a freezer for 20 minutes and put the potato dumplings in a food bag, and keep doing so until all of them have been frozen.

Just throw them in boiling salted water if you want to cook them, without defrosting them first.

ADVICE

If you desire making your potato gnocchi more special, use ingredients for coloring that is for a yellowish color, use turmeric or for red gnocchi with bacon pesto and marjoram, use a hint of tomato concentrate. Whichever color the past is, whether yellow, red or white, it doesn't really matter. What's important is that they aren't new potatoes because these contain much water. It's advisable to use aged potatoes because they are poor in water and rich in starch and to be kneaded, they require less flour.

Garganelli all'Uovo Fatti in Casa (Homemade Egg Garganelli)

Prep time: 60 minutes

Serves: 8

Difficulty: Medium

Cost: Low

Ingredients:

- 100 g durum wheat semolina

- 250 g 00 flour

- Water

- Re-milled semolina for dusting

- 3 eggs

- 2 tbsp. extra virgin olive oil

- Salt to taste

Preparation:

For homemade egg Garganelli you can proceed in two ways:

1. Homemade egg Garganelli first way:

- Make the dough for the garganelli by hand: sift the flours and pour them on a pastry board. Make a hole in the center, where you will break the eggs, add the salt and extra virgin olive oil.

- Start by beating the eggs with a fork, and slowly taking some flour. Then continue to knead with your hands, add a little water (just enough) to obtain a workable dough, but not too soft. Knead until it is smooth and elastic. It will take about 10 minutes. Wrap the dough with plastic wrap and let it rest for at least 1/2 hour.

- After resting, cut the dough in half. The part you don't use right away, keep it wrapped in cling film, and then roll it out later.

- Roll out the dough with a rolling pin, until you get a thin sheet.

- With a wheel cut the dough so as to obtain many squares of about 4 cm each side. Cover them with cling film to keep them from drying out.

- Take one square of pasta at a time, and with the help of the wooden stick, roll it up on itself, starting from the corner. Turn it by pressing lightly on the pastry board, so that the pasta closes well. Pass it on the rigagnocchi. If you have the special tool for garganelli you can train it directly above.

- Remove the garganello from the stick and place it on a dripping pan lined with parchment paper. Proceed in the same way to make all the garganelli.

- You can cook them immediately, or you can keep them for a few days, simply covered with a clean cloth.

2. Homemade egg Garganelli second way

- Make the dough for the Garganelli with the machine: put all the ingredients in the planetary mixer (with the hook) or food processor, and let it go until the dough becomes a smooth and elastic ball.

- Wrap it with plastic wrap and let it rest. Then cut some not too big pieces and pass them several times through the rolls of the pasta machine. Keep on tapering it more and more, increasing or increasing the number, until you reach 5, or better yet 6.

- Then proceed in the same way as to make the garganelli by hand.

Busiate Trapanesi (Busiate from Trapani)

Prep time: 1 hour

Cook time: 5 minutes

Serves: 10

Difficulty: Low

Cost: Very cheap

Ingredients

- 400 ml water

- 2 tbsp. extra virgin olive oil

- 1 kg Durum wheat semolina

- 2 tsp. salt

Preparation:

1. On the wooden pastry board, pour the semolina, in the center, make a bowl and put some little water, oil and salt.

2. Begin kneading by slowly adding the water that is needed. Knead until an elastic and smooth mixture has been obtained. Leave to rest for 1 hour.

3. When you use the planetary mixer, put all ingredients apart from water that is required to be poured slowly slowly. Working on the dough by the planetary mixer takes about 10 minutes for one to get a great result of pasta.

4. It's now time to make the Busiate. Make small rolls from the cut small pasta pieces like thin breadsticks and cut them 10 cm long. Diagonally putting the wooden skewer over the roll end, twist the dough around it and form a curl. By sliding out, remove the Busiate and keep using all the pasta.

Maltagliati

Prep time: 1 hour

Cook time: 2 minutes

Serves: 4

Difficulty: Medium

Cost: Low

Ingredients

- All-purpose flour

- Sea salt

- Water

Preparation:

To make the pasta

1. Use the All-purpose flour to dust the baking sheets.

2. Mix the flour and salt and add water. Use your hands to combine to form dough. Pass the dough through the pasta machine on the widest setting. Use a knife to cut if it becomes very long.

3. Alternatively, you can use a rolling pin to press and make the dough thin.

4. Using a knife cut out your dough into 6-by-4-inch sheets.

5. Dust the pasta sheets with flour and let them rest for 5 minutes so they are not too sticky.

6. Put them one on top of the other (maximum three sheets) and, using a sharp knife, cut the pasta sheets into 1½- to 2-inch irregular shapes resembling a rhombus.

7. Separate the cut pasta and transfer to the baking sheets.

8. Repeat the process until all dough is finished.

Cooking the pasta

1. Bring salted water to boil in a large saucepan. Cook the pasta until al dente, or for 3 minutes. Take a bite to test this.

2. After 3 minutes, use a slotted spoon to remove the pasta and remove the excess water by shaking gently.

3. Serve immediately with the sauce of your choice.

You can use tools and equipment like, Pasta machine or rolling pin, Knife, no serrated, 3 baking sheets, Large pot, Wooden spoon, Slotted spoon

STORAGE

Maltagliati can also be frozen raw. For freezing, put the tray with the Maltagliati in a freezer to harden for some hours. Put them in frost bags when they are well hardened, its better if they are already portioned and return then in the freezer.

When you need to use them, directly boil them from frozen in the boiling water and proceed per the recipe.

Chapter 6: Stuffed Pasta Recipes

Ravioli del Plin

Prep time: 2 hours

Cook time: 1 hour 30 minutes

Serves: 8

Difficulty: Medium

Cost: Medium

Ingredients:

- 4 eggs

- 400 g flour

For the stuffing:

- 1 large onion

- 1 egg

- 30 g spinach

- 200 g pork loin

- 200 g rabbit legs

- 300 g carrots

- 250 g calf pulp

- 100 g celery

- 30 g escarole

- Vegetable broth

- Extra virgin olive oil

- 15 g parmesan cheese

- Salt

- Pepper to taste

Preparation:

1. Put the flour on the work surface and break the eggs inside, one at a time. Mix the eggs using a spoon, starting form the inside. Knead the dough using a fork or with your hands and mix all the flour. If the dough is a bit hard, add few tablespoons of water and continue kneading until its compact and smooth.

2. Using a cling film, cover the pasta and leave it to rest in a cool and dry place for an hour.

3. Cut celery, onions and carrots and set them aside. Remove the veal pulp and the fat part of the loin. You can as well ask the butcher to clean the meat for you by removing the parts that have fats.

4. Heat a few tablespoons of oil in a large saucepan and fry the veal pulp and pork loin until golden brown. Add 2 tablespoons of oil in another pan and fry the rabbit eggs till they are brown.

5. When they are well browned, add the meat, celery, carrots, onions, pepper and salt in a single pan and add water or a ladle of broth. Cover them and cook for 1 hour. If it's necessary, add water or broth during the cooking process.

6. When the meat is ready, remove and let it cool. Keep the cooking juices with the vegetables aside for use in dressing the ravioli. Meanwhile, in a separate pan, add some oil and cook the escarole and spinach until they are wilted. This takes about 5 minutes. If you want, you can cook the endive and spinach in a single pan but first cook the endive for few minutes and add the spinach later since it takes less time.

7. In the meantime, cut the veal meat, pork loin and bone the rabbit into pieces and put all the meats in a mixer. Cut them and add the vegetables, cheese and the egg. Season it with pepper and salt and if it is necessary, add a little broth.

8. Blend all the ingredients together till you get a very compact and dense filling.

9. Now start preparing the ravioli del plin. Take some dough and roll out the thin sheet. On half of the bottom sheet, put half a ball of filling about 20 g and between them, leave a space of 1-2 cm. Quickly work on the dough to avoid it from hardening.

10. Fold the pasta on itself and pinch the edges of the dough on the sides with the fingers, from the long side. Cut the pasta lengthwise few millimeters from the filling using a wheel cut and then separate the ravioli and give it a rectangular shape.

11. Get a tray with a cloth dusted with flour and put the ravioli. Take the previously stewed vegetables and place them in a mixer and blend them till you get a homogeneous and smooth sauce.

12. In abundant salted water, cook the ravioli del plin for few minutes. Drain and season with the sauce obtained from the cooking surface of the meat as soon as they rise to the surface.

13. Serve and enjoy your ravioli del plin.

STORAGE

You can keep the cooked and seasoned plin ravioli in an emetic container in the refrigerator for about 2 days.

You can as well freeze them when they are putting them on a tray that is well-spaced to avoid sticking and you can transfer them to a food bag once they are frozen.

You can cook the plin while its still frozen. Cook them in abundant salted water frozen till they rise to the surface.

If the meat is fresh, the filling can also be frozen.

ADVICE

This is a good dish. You can test it with a sage dressing or classic butter.

If you are following this recipe and the sauce that is roast turns us too liquid, don't worry; let it dry for few minutes on the fire.

Cappelletti

Prep time: 60 minutes

Cook time: 20 minutes

Serves: 6

Difficulty: Medium

Cost: Medium

Ingredients:

For egg pasta:

- 4 eggs

- 400 g 00 flour

For the stuffing:

- 50 g celery

- 60 g carrots

- 150 g pork, minced

- 50 g Parmigiano Reggiano, grated

- 50 g red wine

- 30 g extra virgin olive oil

- 100 g chicken breast

- 100 g veal, minced

- 1 egg

- 60 g golden onions

- Nutmeg

- Black pepper

- Salt

Preparation:

1. Start by preparing the egg pasta. In a large bowl, pour the flour, add the lightly beaten eggs and flour.

2. Use your hands to knead until you get homogeneous and smooth dough, which you will leave to rest at room temperature after wrapping it in a plastic bag for 30 minutes.

3. Meanwhile, be preparing the filling. Cut the carrots, celery and onions and pour in a large pan with oil. Let it stew for like 10 minutes while oftenly stirring.

4. Cut the chicken into tubes and use a knife to chop finely and then add the initial stir-fry with the minced pork and veal.

5. Use a wooden spoon to stir for 6 minutes and then blend with red wine.

6. Once the alcohol evaporates, add the pepper and salt and cook for 4-5 minutes. Pour the meat that is cooked in the mixer and get a mixture that is finer.

7. Transfer the lightly beaten egg and the grated parmesan into a container. Add ground black pepper, salt and nutmeg and then mix. Keep aside.

8. Remove the film and roll out with a rolling pin or a pasta machine after taking the egg pasta. Roll on a lightly floured pastry board. Slightly flatten the dough, flour it lightly and put it between two rollers if you are using a pasta machine.

9. It is crucial to always begin from the widest thickness till you get to the narrow one adding a pinch of flour on each side each time. During this operation, sometimes the dough

deforms and you have to fold it by pulling one flap then the other towards the center.

10. Finally, slightly squeeze in the middle and begin pulling the dough between the rollers again. Get thin sheets of about 0.6 mm and cover them with plastic wraps to avoid drying out as a result of much air

11. Then cut 5 cm squares of dough with a 24 smooth wheel that you will fill with a teaspoon of compound. Try to position the seasoning well by compacting it in the center and fold the opposite end and form a triangle. Pull the two ends towards you and join them.

12. Flatten down and join them slightly pinching with your fingers. Since they tend to open while you are cooking, make sure they are closed tightly. Repeat this operation for all the others until you get all the cappelletti ready to be cooked.

13. While you prepare them, lay them on a tray where you will have put a lightly floured dish and clean cloth with semolina.

STORAGE

If you have used fresh ingredients, cappelletti can be frozen. Just place them on a tray while they are kept apart, put the tray in a freezer for about 30 minutes.

Once they have hardened very well, but it's better if they are portioned already, put them in frost bags and take them back to the freezer.

When you need to use them, directly boil them from frozen in boiling water and continue as per the recipe.

ADVICE

During processing, if the dough gets so dry, you can use water to brush the surface of pasta disks.

You can replace the 3 types of minced meat with what you prefer.

Caramelle Ricotta e Spinaci (Ricotta and Spinach Candies)

Prep time: 90 minutes

Cook time: 20 minutes

Serves: 4

Difficulty: Easy

Cost: Low

Ingredients:

For egg pasta:

- 2 eggs

- 250 g 00 flour

- 1 yolk

For the stuffing:

- 1 pinch, nutmeg

- 250 g spinach

- 50 g Parmigiano Reggiano

- 125 g cow's milk ricotta

- Black pepper

- Salt

For the dressing

- Parmesan cheese

- 6 leaves, sage

- 100 g butter

Preparation:

1. Preparing the ricotta and spinach candies, you start with egg pasta. In a bowl, pour the flour and keep about 50 g to add if need be, add eggs and do everything inside one bowl. Once the eggs are absorbed, continue handling the dough on a work surface until its elastic and smooth.

2. Give it a spherical shape once they are ready and let them rest in a cook place with lights on for 30 minutes after wrapping them in a plastic wrap.

3. To prepare the filling, in a non-stick pan, put very little salt water, boil the spinach or simply sauté them on low heat or cook them in the steam. Squeeze and chop them finely. The spinach will weigh 100 gr once cooked and well squeezed.

4. In a bowl, put the chopped spinach in which you will add the parmesan and ricotta, salt, pepper and nutmeg. Use a soft but compact mixture to mix all the ingredients.

5. In a very thin sheet, roll out the egg pasta which you will cut into rectangles measuring 10x8 cm. Put a little teaspoon of filling in every rectangle of pasta and on a longer side, wrap the dough on itself.

6. Model your sweets by turning the left flap counterclockwise and the right flap clockwise as though to close the paper of the candy. Using a serrated wheel cut the outer edges of both edges.

7. After modeling all the candies, put them to dry on a floured work surface for an hour. In salted boiling water, cook the pasta for at least 5 minutes.

8. Let the sage leaves gild in melted butter in a pan.

9. Drain the candies once cooked and season them with sage and butter and grated parmesan to taste.

10. Your spinach and ricotta candies are ready to be served.

STORAGE

Ricotta and spinach candies can be kept in a refrigerator for one day.

You can alternatively freeze them raw. To freeze, put the candies on the tray in the freezer for them to harden for some hours. Put them in frost bags once they are well hardened and take them back to the freezer.

If you need to use them, directly boil them from frozen in boiling water per the recipe.

ADVICE

Pack the candies as soon as you pull the dough when it's still workable and wet since it tends to quickly dry out otherwise it will make the filling to leak out because it will break in the twisting process.

Casoncelli

Prep time: 60 minutes

Serves: 6

Difficulty: Medium

Cost: Medium

Ingredients:

For egg pasta:

- 165 g medium, eggs

- 300 g 00 flour

For the stuffing:

- 150 g, Veal, ground

- 150 g Pork, ground

- 20 g Parmigiano Reggiano, grated

- 150 g Chard

- 15 g Macaroons

- 10 g Extra virgin olive oil

- 30 g Breadcrumbs

- 20 g Raisins

- 3 g Parsley

Preparation:

1. Begin by preparing the fresh egg pasta to make the casoncelli. In a large bowl, put the flour and keep aside like 50 g to add if needed basing on how much the eggs absorb.

2. Pout the slightly beaten eggs in the hole with a classic fountain shape that you made in the center.

3. Begin using your hands to knead. Fist in a bowl and when the dough is consistent, transfer to the pastry board. Continue kneading vigorously until you get quite elastic and firm dough.

4. Form a ball and line it with a cling film and let it rest for 30 minutes at room temperature. After this, it will be easier to spread and more elastic.

5. Meanwhile, start filling. Rinse the raisins under running water and for them to soften soak them in hot water for about 10 minutes. In the meantime, wash the beets, check the stem base and cut the leaves roughly. In the bottom of

the pan, heat a little oil and put the beets to stew. On low heat, allow them to dry. This takes few minutes.

6. Put the minced pork and beef in a glass mixer and add the breadcrumbs, Grana, the cooked chard and the whole amaretti and operate the blades by chopping until you get a fine compound. Add the grated parsley and lemon zest and lastly the well-drained and softened raisins.

7. Do the seasoning with pepper and salt and mix to obtain a homogeneous mixture, which can be transferred to a sac-a-poche. Recover the rested egg pasta, divide it into smaller loaves and with the help of the knuckle, roll the dough until you get 1 mm thick sheets. To get about 21 cm wide strips, cut the sheet length wise.

8. To keep them well-spaced from each other with the sac-a-poche distributed along the strip of the walnuts that are stuffed, using s damp brush or by sprinkling, wet the pasta with water around the stuffing to make it more adhesive. Fold the upper edge of the strip after collecting it, over the stuffing nuts and wit finer pressure, make them adhere and so that the bubbles don't form inside your casoncelli, make sure that you let the air escape.

9. Equipping yourself with a 6 cm diameter festooned pastry ring and to ensure the shape of a crescent, keep half of it out and to form your ravioli, cop pate. Use a little water to moist them and pinch the ravioli with the filling. Fold them towards the semicircle edge.

10. Adhere to the moistened dough to form the casoncelli by exerting slight pressure. Continue like this until both the filling and the dough are exhausted and when they are ready, let the casoncelli rest on a floured tray before cooking for 25-30 minutes.

11. Cook the casoncelli in salted boiling water for 6 minutes. Season as you like one its drained.

STORAGE

Casoncelli can be kept in an airtight container in a fridge for a maximum of 2 days.

You can freeze them while raw for at least a month and you can directly cook them in boiling water without thawing them first.

ADVICE

casoncelli can be seasoned by skipping in a pan after cooking them with sage, butter and diced bacon.

Mezzelune al Salmone ed Erba Cipollina (Salmon and Chives Mezzelune)

Prep time: 60 minutes

Cook time: 6 minutes

Serves: 4

Difficulty: Medium

Cost: Medium

Ingredients:

400 g Pasta, fresh (the recipe is at the beginning of the book)

For the filling:

- 2 tbsps. Chives

- 400 g Cow's milk ricotta

- 300 g Salmon, smoked

- Salt

- Pepper

For the dressing:

- 2 tbsp. Chives

- 100 g butter

Preparation

1. Prepare the egg pasta per the recipe.

2. Use a knife to chop the salmon, put in a bowl and add 2 tablespoons of chopped chives, little freshly ground pepper and ricotta and add salt. Adjust if necessary.

3. Use a pasta machine or by hand, roll the egg pasta and form a sheet as thin as possible and make discs with a diameter of at least 5 cm with the help of a round pastry cutter.

4. On each disc, put a little filling and form a crescent by closing it on yourself and to weld the edges, lightly press them. Moist the edges with water if the paste doesn't stick well when using a brush.

5. In pan with much salted water, cook the crescents and also melt the butter in a pan.

6. Drain the crescents and sprinkle with chopped chives and season them with melted butter.

7. Serve the salmon crescents while hot.

ADVICE

You can season the crescents with cream, a light and fluid bechamel sauce that is flavored with chives or with salmon.

Tortellini

Prep time: 150 minutes

Cook time: 10 minutes

Serves: 6

Difficulty: Medium

Cost: Medium

Ingredients:

For egg pasta:

- 400g 00 flour

- 4 eggs

For the stuffing:

- 70 g Pork loin

- 80 g Parma raw ham

- 70 g Beef veal pulp

- 150 g Parmesan cheese to be grated

- 1 large egg

- 80 g Bologna Mortadella

- 20 g Butter

- Nutmeg

- Black pepper to taste

- Salt to taste

Preparation:

1. In preparing the tortellini, begin with preparing the egg pasta. Add the flour on a pastry board and form a hole at the middle and then add the eggs. Use a fork to break eggs and start incorporating. Switch to using your hands and keep kneading to get a smooth and soft dough. Use a cling film to cover and allow a minimum of 30 minutes to rest.

2. Meanwhile get the filling ready: cut the pork loin and veal meat in coarse pieces and place the aside. Repeat with mortadella and raw ham.

3. Add butter to a pan and melt it and add the meat. Cook it for 10 minutes until it is brown. Allow it to cool and add the

meat, mortadella and raw ham to a mixer. Blend until well mixed. Add pepper, nutmeg, parmesan and egg and blend further to form a dough. Place the pasta in a pasta machine and roll it out into a thin sheet; you can alternatively use a rolling pin.

4. Cut 4cm thick squares from the dough using a sharp knife or cutter wheel. Ensure the remaining pasta is always covered. Put some few grams of the filling and make the tortellini. Fold a square to a triangular shape and press edges to stick them.

5. Fold the triangle's base upwards. Rest the resulting dough on your index finger, the triangle tip looking up. Join together the ends using some pressure and turn them down to make the edges fit.

6. Lay the tortellini on cloth that is floured lightly. Repeat till all ingredients are finished. Place the tortellini in a cloth that is floured and you can proceed to cooing in meat broth.

STORAGE

Freeze each tortellini while separated for half an hour. Put them together and freeze.

Allow them to dry if you cannot freeze them. Put them in a closed in a container and put in a fridge, either cooked or raw.

ADVICE

Cook the tortellini strictly in meat broth and serve with the broth.

You can use the meat that you prefer e.g. pork, turkey, or chicken.

Ravioli di Ricotta (Ricotta Ravioli)

Prep time: 60
minutes

Serves: 24

Difficulty: Medium

Cost: Low

Ingredients:

For egg pasta:

- 2 large eggs

- 250 g 00 flour

- 1 yolk

- Durum wheat semolina

For the stuffing:

- 20 g Grana Padano to be grated

- 400 g Cows milk ricotta

- Nutmeg to taste

- Black pepper

- Salt to taste

Preparation:

1. You begin by preparing the egg pasta. Add flour to a bowl and add the eggs. Vigorously knead the ingredients to form a smooth and homogenous mixture. Add flour if need be. You can also add some water, little by little, if it is too dry.

2. Move the dough to a flour-dusted work surface and use a cling film to cover the dough. Allow about 30 minutes to rest at room temperature.

3. Meanwhile you can be filling as the dough rests. Get a bowl and season with pepper and salt. Add thyme leaves, combine with the ricotta.

4. Move the mixture into a sac-à-poche and refrigerate. The pasta will have rested enough. Divide it into equal halves. Take one half and leave the other one covered. Use re-milled semolina flour to flour the first half of the dough and roll it through the pasta machine in the widest setting to get a 2mm-thick sheet. Place the sheet on a flour-dusted work

surface. Repeat with the remaining dough. Create rectangular pieces and arrange them 3cm apart.

5. Drizzle water on the sheet's edges or use a kitchen brush to brush with ravioli. Match the edges and press them together using your fingers to remove air.

6. Use a notched cutter wheel or a sharp knife to make the ravioli starting at filling to another, 4x4 cm. Flour a tray and arrange the ravioli there. The ravioli is now ready for cooking.

STORAGE

You can freeze the ricotta ravioli up to a maximum of one month. Harden the ravioli by placing them while still on a tray in a freezer for two hours. Set them in frost bags and return them to a freezer.

ADVICE

You can use other herbs such as dill or parsley to personalize the filling.

Tortelli di Zucca (Pumpkin Tortelli)

Prep time: 150 minutes

Cook time: 20 minutes

Serves: 4

Difficulty: Difficult

Cost: Medium

Ingredients:

For egg pasta:

- 104 g eggs

- 200 g 00 flour

For the stuffing:

- 160 g Macaroons

- 170 g Pear valance mustard

- 52 g eggs

- 500 g pumpkin

- 65 g Parmigiano Reggiano, grated

- Salt to taste

- Nutmeg to be grated

Preparation:

1. Prepare the filling and put it in the fridge to rest overnight for a flavorful mix. Cut the pumpkin into slices and put them on a parchment-lined pan.

2. Bake for 20 minutes at 220° in a preheated oven, while occasionally pricking using a fork. The result should be a soft pumpkin. Add the amaretti in a bowl as the pumpkin cooks and use your hands to crumble them.

3. Use a knife to chop the pear valance mustard. When the pumpkin is ready, rest it in the oven to cool. This also allows it to dry and loose water. Use a spoon to scoop the pulp and add it into a potato masher and set a small bowl to collect.

4. Add the amaretti and the mustard to the pulp and use a spatula to mix.

5. Add in cheese and egg and thoroughly mix. Add salt and the nutmeg. Use a plastic wrap to cover and refrigerate it overnight, or 24 hours.

6. Prepare the pasta: pour the flour on pastry board and scoop a well at the middle. Break in the egg and use a fork to incorporate. Switch to using hands and mix to get smooth and soft dough. Add water if the dough is too dry and if it is too sticky, add some flour. Do this until you obtain smooth dough. Form the dough into a spherical shape. Use a cling film to cover the dough.

7. Allow a minimum of 30 minutes for the dough to rest at room temperature. After the time has elapsed, divide the dough into two. Leave one half covered in the cling film and put the other through the pasta machine or using a rolling pin. Roll the dough to get 1mm thick rectangles.

8. Dust a work surface with flour and roll the dough on top. Use a pastry cutter to level the dough and get strips of 9cm width. Put the strip on the filling piles in the top part while you space the piles, on the pasta strip. Cover the filling by folding the pasta strip: brush the pastry with water if it is a bit dry.

9. Use a wheel cutter to cut shape and size you desire. The tortelli size and shape vary depending on traditions and one's personal preference. Proceed till all pasta is finished. If you wish, you can cook, as your tortelli is ready.

STORAGE

Freeze the tortelli and when it becomes hard, put in a frost bag and put it back in a freezer for storage.

ADVICE

For filling that is less sweet, use mature cheese or you can add more salt to balance. You can use sage and butter to season your tortelli as this combo enhances the filling flavor. You can have it with a tomato sauce or a sausage ragout if you want a taste that is decisive. You can as well bring in cooked seasonal vegetables to get a unique dish.

CONCLUSION

The art of making pasta has a history of hundreds of years, do not expect to make masterpieces at the first attempt but continue to practice cooking even more delicious pasta dishes

The art of making pasta has a history of hundreds of years, do not expect to make masterpieces at the first attempt but continue to practice cooking even more delicious pasta dishes

When walking through the refrigerator case of the grocery store, you might see one of those clear plastic cases of pasta that is labeled as being "Fresh" and be tempted to grab it. The reality is these shouldn't be called fresh pasta. It's just that "Premade soft pasta product" doesn't exactly roll off the tongue.

Most of the time, these prepackaged versions are made with dough stabilizers and other additives to help them keep longer in grocery store cases. Many of these additives keep the pasta from interacting with the sauce. The pasta tends to slide around in the sauce like two strangers instead of forming a harmonious relationship with it.

The price for these packages of premade pasta is usually very high when compared to the cheap price of rolling out fresh pasta made from flour and eggs at home.

Fresh pasta made at home and often finished in the sauce has the ability to form a relationship with the sauce in a way that benefits both components. The process is actually rather easy once you understand the principles of making and rolling it out. All at the cost of around a dollar!

This homemade pasta cookbook seeks to rekindle an art that has been practiced by mankind for many centuries, but with the advent of modernization, this art is slowly losing its shine and place in our modern kitchens and culinary practice.

There are a lot of different kinds of pasta around the world and exist many ways of its cooking and preparing. This cookbook features pasta dough illustrating the ease of making the dough and the ingredients you would require making the dough.

The cookbook also highlights stuffed, short and long pastas with amazing results.

After the pastas are cooked and ready to be enjoyed, it is important to understand how best to enjoy the meal.

Pasta dishes as alluded to earlier are indeed dishes that are enjoyed widely across different regions of the world and on many dining tables in homes across the world.

The popularity of pasta dishes, either as an appetizer, side dish, an ingredient in soups, as a main course or even as a dessert, cannot be over emphasized.

The ease of putting a pasta-based meal and pulling it off probably has a lot to do with its popularity. One thing that is not in question though, is the love of pasta even among different social groups of persons and across all ages.

Pasta is an appealing and tasty delicacy and is extremely enjoyable to eat, put together and combine with almost all types of food classes enjoyed by mankind.

Pasta Sauces Cookbook

The Most Delicious and Tasty Recipes to Cook Typical Pasta Dishes of Italian Cuisine

Owen Conti

Introduction

Food is so important, the more you think of it. Over food is where relationships blossom, it is an opportunity to leave a lasting legacy, a chance to feel connected to those that have passed or who live far away. Food is a connection, most of the best memories we hold dear to us, there was more than likely food involved.

This in essence, is what pasta is all about. The way we cut our vegetables, treat the food we prepare is inherited, it is taught and then transferred to the next generation. The art of food and the cooking thereof is a sensory experience that adheres to what is freshly available at the time and honoring it in the dish that is then subsequently prepared.

Who doesn't love pasta sauce? Pasta sauce recipes can make even the most boring Italian dish taste absolutely incredible. There are literally over 100 different types of pasta sauce recipes that you can make to accompany nearly every kind of Italian dish that you want to make. Pasta sauce can be served with virtually any dish ranging from homemade pasta, to pizza to even dessert dishes.

This book is a combination of classic and traditional recipes paired with more contemporary, Italian inspired meals that suit those who have limited time to cook but adore whipping up something to eat. The recipes can be adapted to suit your tastes and needs, the beauty of cooking is that it is a chance for you to experiment, add, subtract and substitute.

Chapter 1: The Soffritto: The First Step for the Perfection of Many Sauces

Tips to Make the Perfect Sauté

The Container

It is good and necessary to have a non-stick pan that has edges, which are high enough to prevent the splashing of ingredients out and also to avoid having to scrape the vegetables. This helps to bring the sauté to regular cooking.

The Bottom of the Pan: Margarine, Butter or Oil?

This is quite a big dilemma for a lot of people: extra virgin oil is rigorously used to prepare the sauté because it is genuine and its flavor is unmistakable. There is however not enough necessary to increase the doses: you need self-control and this you measure a spoonful of oil as per the number of people present. When your pour it on the pan, avoid preheating because there will be a nullification of the health-giving properties of the oil. Cook it over medium heat when cold.

How to Select Vegetables?

Sautéed Vegetables

The vegetables are selected depending on the flavor that you would wish to have from the sauté. There are those that prefer onions, others prefer shallot, others both or the leek: For a savory and delicate taste at the ideal point, common for fish and sauces, risotto, go with onions, and they should be compact and small. Carrots are ideal when short and also take a short time to soften them when cooking. Groom your celery: wash them in running water starting with the filaments. Remove a cm of the original part and the cut it into strips, and then lengthwise and then widthwise.

How to Chop the Ingredients?

In order to get a sauté with a flavor, which is almost impeccable, more delicate, and leaves just authentic flavor to the braised or sauce, you need to chop the ingredients finely.

It should be a fast tool that is convenient, but you should not at any time chop the vegetables using a mixer: when the blades of the mixer rotate, they give off heat which changes the flavor of the ingredients and this will be perceived when cooking. The knife or the classic grater is fine for the skilled ones, they key thing is that you have to manually mince.

Cooking

Make sure that you keep on turning continuously when you gently sew the vegetables in the oil. How long should it take you cooking? You just need to observe the onion's color and consistency: when it turns golden and soft, and can almost melt in your mouth, you can be sure that it is ready.

Now you are good to go! Make a perfect sauté that will be full of flavors for your dishes.

How to Make the Sauté

Prep time: 15 minutes

Cook time: 15 minutes

Serves: 3

Difficulty: Very easy

Cost: Very low

Ingredients:

- 1 white onion

- 1 rib celery

- Extra virgin olive oil to taste

- 1 carrot

- 50 ml White wine

Preparation:

1. In preparing the sauté, you require a small knife and a potato peeler. Peel and divide into half. On the cutting board, put the part that is flat and begin cutting the first half in slices in length and then width in order to get cubes.

2. Go to the carrots. Use a small knife to remove the carrot ends. Peel the carrot using a peeler and then wash it under running water.

3. Cut the carrot in thin slices lengthwise and divide them in half and to get cubes, finally cut them transversely.

4. Under running water, wash the stick well and then remove the external leaves on the top and the lateral ones. Use the potato pillar to remove the external filamentous membrane. Divide the rib in half and cut it in many strips and then cut the strips into cubes that are small.

5. On a pan, put extra virgin olive oil, heat and then add the celery, carrots and chopped onions. Turn all vegetables on all sides to brown and cook until the onion has become transparent or for at least 15 minutes. You can as well use water or white wine to blend after 5 minutes in order to speed the cooking.

STORAGE

If you prepare a fair amount, the sauté can be frozen. Use a clean tea towel to dry it very well and put it in a bag for freezing.

Chapter 2: Meat Sauces

Ragout

Prep time: 7 minutes

Cook time: 60 minutes

Ingredients:

- 200 gr beef pulp

- 1 onion

- 1 carrot

- 200 gr tomato pulp

- 1 celery heart, cubed

To taste:

- Extra virgin olive oil

- White wine

- Pepper

- Salt

Preparation:

1. To make tomato sauce with meat sauce, fry the onion, celery and carrot in little extra virgin olive oil.

2. Add the beef twice to the vegies, add pepper and salt and drizzle in some white wine.

3. Add in the fresh tomato pulp into a pan and cook for about 50-60 minutes.

4. Boil filled pasta, noodles, and wheat semolina pasta of choice in salted water. Season it when ready with the meat sauce and enjoy.

Bolognese Ragout

Prep time: 20 minutes

Cook time: 210 minutes

Serves: 4

Difficulty: Easy

Cost: Low

Ingredients:

- 250 g Ground pork, very fatty

- 1 tbsp Extra virgin olive oil

- 500 g Coarse ground beef

- 250 g Tomato sauce

- 40 g Whole milk

- 50 g Golden onions, thinly sliced

- 50 g Carrots, peeled and chopped

- 50 g Celery, finely chopped

- 250 g White wine

- 3 liters Water

- Salt

- Black pepper

Preparation:

1. Peel and chop the onion, carrot and celery. Get 50 g off each one of the ingredients.

2. Add oil to a saucepan and then add in the chopped onion, carrot and celery and sauté on low heat for 10 minutes while occasionally stirring. After 10 minutes, or when the sauté is withered, add the ground pork and the coarsely ground beef.

3. Cook them slowly until brown, or for about 10 minutes while occasionally stirring. At first, all juices will come out but will dry with time. Add in the white wine and blend. When the whine evaporates and it is dry pour in the tomato puree. Add in 1 liter of water and salt. Stir and cook for about 60 minutes on medium-low heat.

4. After 60 minutes, add in another liter of water, stir, cover and cook for 60 more minutes. This way, the ragu cooks for a minimum of 3 hours. The end result is very dry. Season

with pepper and salt and turn the heat off. Pour in the milk and mix and your sauce is ready.

STORAGE

The Bolognese ragu can be prepared earlier and you heat it when it's time to eat.

Store it in cling covered film glass container for about 2-3 days.

You can also freeze if you want.

ADVICE

There are many traditions that are associated with the Bolognese sauce recipe.

The pork should be very fatty called pancetta in jargon. The bovine one should be coarse grained for the rustic consistency of the ragù.

The sauce doesn't have to be much as some people believe. A restricted amount of sauce is therefore used to season the tagliatelle unlike lasagna, which requires a sauce that is soft.

The purpose of the milk is making the ragù creamy and more full-embodied.

Carbonara

Prep time: 15 minutes

Cook time: 10 minutes

Serves: 4

Difficulty: Easy

Cost: Low

Ingredients:

- 6 Medium egg yolks
- 50 g Roman pecorino
- 320 g Spaghetti
- 150 g Pillow
- Black pepper to taste
- Salt to taste

Preparation:

1. Add salted water to a pot for cooking the pasta. In the meantime, slice and cut the pillow rind into strips of 1-2 cm. The rind can be used again in flavoring other preps. Add into a nonstick pan and cook over medium heat for about 15 minutes. Be careful, otherwise you could burn it.

2. Meanwhile, put the spaghetti in salted boiling water and cook as per the package instructions. In the meantime, add

the egg yolks into a bowl and add in pecorino and make sure that you leave some to garnish the pasta.

3. Use black pepper to season and use a hand whisk to mix everything. To dilute the mixture, add a spoon of water.

4. By now, the pillow will be ready. Turn the heat off and set it aside to rest. Drain the pasta al dente directly onto the pan with guanciale and fry it for a short time in order to flavor it. Take the pan off the heat and add in the pecorino and eggs mixture and stir.

5. You can add some little water to make it creamy. Serve the carbonara flavoring with pecorino and seasoning with the black pepper.

STORAGE

It is not recommended to store the spaghetti carbonara. You should eat it immediately.

ADVICE

In order to enrich the spaghetti carbonara you need to respect your tastes in the kitchen. For example, you can alternatively use rigatoni instead of spaghetti or use half sleeves in the place of bacon. You can use grated parmesan to replace pecorino. You can add a combination of yolks and whole eggs to the pasta or you can add some little water.

Gricia

Prep time: 10 minutes

Cook time: 15 minutes

Serves: 4

Difficulty: Easy

Cost: Medium

Ingredients:

- 60 g Roman pecorino cheese, grated
- 250 g Guanciale, already peppered
- 320 g Rigatoni
- Salt to taste

Preparation:

1. Fill a pan with salted water and place it on heat; it will be used to cook the pasta. Slice the bacon into 1 cm-thick slices. Remove any rind present and separate. The separated rind can be stored in a refrigerator and be used again. The strips you get will be of thickness of about ½ cm. Add bacon to the hot pan on medium heat and do not add other fats.

2. Allow it to sizzle until they turn crispy and golden brown, or for about 10 minutes and watch out not to burn. Meanwhile, the water should have boiled by now. Add the pasta in and cook. As the pasta cooks, finely grate the pecorino. About 2 minutes from the pasta being cooked, add a ladle of pasta to slow down the pillow cooking. Shake the pan.

3. The pasta is done cooking at this time. Drain it into the sauce and keep the water. Sauté as you stir and shake the pan for 1 minute and then get the pan off the heat. Drizzle with 1/3 of the pecorino cheese. Add some more water as you may need.

4. Sauté the pasta as you stir. Serve pasta on Gricia and use the pecorino that remained to garnish.

STORAGE

It is advised that you eat immediately. If you want to store, you can put it into the fridge for up to 24 hours. You should not freeze.

ADVICE

As you cook bacon, do it in a pan that is already hot while regularly checking to ensure that it does not burn. If your bacon is peppered externally, make sure you add black pepper that is grated to taste.

Tomato Sauce with Meatballs

Prep time: 30 minutes

Cook time: 80 minutes

Serves: 4

Difficulty: Very easy

Cost: Low

Ingredients:

- 320 g Spaghetti

- 30 g Extra virgin olive oil

- 20 g Shallot

- 700 g Tomato sauce

- 1 clove Garlic, peeled

- Salt to taste

For Meatballs:

- 50 g PDO Parmesan Cheese

- 100 g Luganega

- 100 g minced pork

- 50 g Whole-meal bread only the crumb holds

- 80 g Mortadella in a single slice

- Nutmeg to taste

- 5 g Chopped parsley

- 1 medium Egg

- Salt to taste

- Black pepper to taste

Preparation:

1. Make the sauce first. Chop the shallot finely and fry it on low heat. Add in the garlic and keep on frying for about 6 minutes.

2. Pour in the tomato puree, add pepper, salt and cover and cook for a minimum of 0 minutes. Meanwhile as you cook the sauce, prepare the meatballs: blend together the mortadella and the whole-meal bread without crusts in a mixer.

3. Use a sharp knife to cut the casing off the sausage and chop it. Chop the parsley finely too.

4. Pour in the sausage, breadcrumbs with the mortadella and the pork in a large bowl.

5. Add parsley, pepper and salt.

6. Add grated nutmeg to flavor, grated cheese and egg.

7. Use your hands to knead all ingredients until they mix well. Use a plastic wrap to cover and allow about 15 minutes to rest in the refrigerator.

8. Remove the meatball dough and form 10 g balls until all the dough is finished.

9. When the sauce is cooked, eliminate garlic and add in the meatballs into the sauce. Cook on low heat for about half an hour.

10. Boil salted water in a saucepan and add in the pasta. Drain it al dente and work on sauce. Add the meatballs with spaghetti and your recipe is good to go.

STORAGE

It is advised that you eat spaghetti with freshly made meatballs. You can store the meatball sauce in a refrigerator for about 2-3 days.

ADVICE

You can make the meatball sauce a day earlier to enable better mixing of the flavors, if you so wish.

Boscaiola

Prep time: 30 minutes

Cook time: 25 minutes

Serves: 4

Difficulty: Very easy

Cost: High

Ingredients:

- 400 g Porcini mushrooms
- 60 g White onions, chopped
- 30 g Liquid fresh cream
- 200 g Smoked bacon
- 320 g Pennette Rigate
- 40 g Extra virgin olive oil
- 400 g Tomato sauce
- Black pepper to taste
- Salt to taste
- Parsley to taste

Preparation:

1. Wash the mushrooms, using a small knife to remove excess soil. Use a brush or a dampened cloth to remove any remaining soil. Cut the mushrooms into ½ cm layers.

2. Bring water with salt to boil in a pan. Meanwhile, slice the bacon into 4 cm cubes.

3. Heat 20 g Extra virgin olive oil in a pan over high heat and fry the bacon while frequently stirring. After a few minutes, it will be ready. Set it aside.

4. In the same pan used to fry the bacon, add the remaining oil and put in the chopped onion. Sauté until the onion has dried and the add in the mushrooms. Sauté while occasionally stirring for about 6 minutes until brown.

5. Pour in the tomato puree and the cook for 6-9 minutes on low heat. As soon as it shrinks, add in the bacon that was kept aside and cook for about 5 minutes. In the meantime, begin to cook pasta and you will drain it al dente.

6. Add cream to the dressing with the fire on low heat and mix by stirring. Chop the parsley.

7. Drain the penne straight in the pan and stir. Season with salt, pepper and chopped parsley and then stir. The recipe is now ready for consumption.

STORAGE

You can store penne alla Boscaiola in a refrigerator for just one day, but do not forget that the consistency of the sauce and the pasta could be affected.

ADVICE

Pennette alla Boscaiola can be enjoyed differently in various places. This means that you can vary the ingredients you use depending on where you come from.

Amatriciana

Prep time: 10 minutes

Cook time: 25 minutes

Serves: 4

Difficulty: Easy

Cost: Low

Ingredients:

- 150 g Pillow of Amatrice

- 400 g Peeled tomatoes

- 320 g Spaghetti

- 50 g White wine

- Extra virgin olive oil to taste

- 75 g Roman pecorino cheese for grating

- 1 Fresh chili

- Salt to taste

Preparation:

1. Bring salted water to boil for cooking the pasta. Meanwhile, go to the seasoning: remove the rind from the pillow and slice it into 1 cm thick slices. Cut the slices into ½ cm strips.

2. In a steel pan, heat the oil and add bacon strips and chili. Cook on low heat for about 6-8 minutes until it is crispy brown and the fat turns transparent. Ensure that you stir occasionally so as to avoid burning it. Add in the white wine to blend with the melted fat and increase the heat until it evaporates.

3. Remove the bacon strips and put them in a plate and set aside. Add in tomatoes to the pan: use your hands to fray them directly in the cooking base. Cook for about 8-9 minutes. The water in the pan should have boiled at this point; add in spaghetti and cook al dente.

4. Meanwhile add salt, eliminate red pepper from sauce, add bacon strips and mix to combine.

5. Drain the spaghetti straight to the pan containing the sauce as soon as they are cooked. Quickly sauté the pasta so that it mixes well with the sauce. Turn the heat off if you prefer the pasta al dente or otherwise add some little water and

go on cooking the pasta. Drizzle the grated pecorino and your recipe is ready for consumption.

STORAGE

You can store Spaghetti Amatriciana in a fridge in a container that is airtight for up to one day. You are advised to refrain from freezing.

ADVICE

For a different taste variety of this recipe, you can try it with onion or garlic or blending using water in place of wine.

Pappardelle with Hare

Prep time: 30 minutes

Cook time: 265 minutes

Serves: 4

Difficulty: Medium

Cost: Low

Ingredients:

- 500 g hare, ground
- 350 g tomato sauce
- 200 g water
- 250 g egg pappardelle
- 3 leaves laurel
- 50 g carrots
- 50 g white onions
- 50 g celery
- 1 clove, garlic
- 15 g, extra virgin olive oil

- Salt

- 1 sprig rosemary

- 50 g red wine

- 1 pinch black pepper

Preparation:

Begin making the ragu. Wash the carrots and celery. Remove the celery from the external filaments and peel the onion, carrot and garlic. Divide it in half and remove the soul and cut the remaining finely.

1. Add the oil, the chopped celery, carrot, onion and garlic and put on heat. Stir for about 5-7 minutes.

2. Add the ground hare meat when the sauté is ready, put over medium heat and stir gently for 4-5 minutes.

3. Add the chopped bay leaves and rosemary after the meat has changed the color, blend with red wine and raise the flame a little.

4. Continue stirring until the part that is alcoholic has fully evaporated. Lower the heat and season with pepper and salt. Pour in the water, tomato puree and mix again.

5. Use a lid to cover the ragu and over medium heat, allow it to cook for like 4 hours and to make sure it doesn't stick on the bottom, mix occasionally. Transfer to a large pan once it's ready.

6. Cook the pappardelle in much boiling water and add salt to taste. Trough the pasta and pour it in a large pan where you transferred the ragu.

7. Just mix everything together and serve your pappardelle with the hare while still hot.

STORAGE

Pappardelle with hare are good if eaten immediately they are ready. You can keep the ragu in the refrigerator if left over for like a maximum of 2-3 days closed in an airtight container. An alternative, you can freeze it if you have used all the fresh ingredient.

ADVICE

If you prepare the ragu a day before, all the different flavors merge together and give life to an appealing ragu. You can cool the ragu at room temperature and store it in a fridge once its cooked.

Orecchiette Broccoli e Salsiccia

(Orecchiette Broccoli and Sausage)

Prep time: 20 minutes

Cook time: 15 minutes

Serves: 4

Difficulty: Very easy

Cost: Low

Ingredients:

- 300 g Broccoli

- 40 g White wine

- 2 Thyme sprigs

- 320 g Orecchiette

- 300 g Sausage

- 1 Garlic clove

- 30 g Extra virgin olive oil

- 1 sprig rosemary

- Salt to taste

- Black pepper to taste

Preparation:

1. In making the orecchiette with sausage and broccoli, begin with boiling a pot full of salted water. Remove the broccoli tops and divide them in halves even when they are very large.

2. Transfer them to the pan in boiling water and put a lid on it. Cook the vegetables for about 7 minutes.

3. In the meantime, chop the rosemary and the thyme finely and put them aside. Remove the casing after cutting the sausage and use your hands to gently pull it away and then using the prongs of the fork, shell the sausage.

4. Use olive oil to sprinkle a large pan and you fry the garlic clove and then add the sausage. Add the chopped aromatic herbs after few seconds and bled with meat together with white wine.

5. Without throwing away the cooking water, use a skimmer to remove the cooked broccoli and keep adding them to the meat little by little. Allow them to cook for 4 minutes and

then use the kitchen tongs to remove the garlic and add a pinch of black pepper.

6. Allow the water where you cooked the broccoli to reach a boil and then toss the pasta and cook it. Use a skimmer to drain when the pasta has cooked and directly transfer it to the sausage dressing and the broccoli.

7. Take the ladle of cooking water where it's necessary and add the last orecchiette and then mix the pasta in the seasoning well and add black pepper. In a pan, sauté everything well for some minutes.

8. The orecchiette with sausage and broccoli are now ready. Serve and enjoy.

STORAGE

You can store the broccoli and sausage dressing for 1 day in the refrigerator but you should first close it in an airtight container. Once you add the orecchiette, its advisable that you immediately consume them

ADVICE

For the dressing, you can add finely chopped chili pepper in order to give a nice spicy note to the dish.

Penne al Baffo (Penne alla Whisker)

Prep time: 5 minutes

Cook time: 12 minutes

Serves: 4

Difficulty: Easy

Cost: Low

Ingredients:

- 100 g Sliced cooked ham
- 25 g Tomato sauce
- 320 g Whole Wheat Mezze Penne Rigate
- Parsley to taste
- Extra virgin olive oil to taste
- 300 g Fresh liquid cream
- Black pepper to taste
- Salt to taste

Preparation:

1. For making the mustache pens, begin by washing them, allow them to dry and chop the parsley finely and set them aside and go to cooked ham and also cut it in thin strips.

2. Put a pan with plenty of water on the fire when it has been salted to taste. This will be used for pasta cooking.

193

3. Go to seasoning making, into the pan, pour a drizzle of oil and add the ham. Allow it to brown for at least 1 minute and as well add the cream. Mix everything together and then on low heat, add the tomato puree and cook them for 10 minutes.

4. Meanwhile, cook the pasta and then drain it al dente and directly transfer it to the pan with the dressing. Use pepper and salt to season and add the chopped parsley.

5. Mix everything well and then serve your penne pasta while it is still hot.

STORAGE

It's recommended to consume the whisker pens immediately.

You can alternatively keep them in the refrigerator for a day while closed in an airtight container. It's not recommended to freeze.

ADVICE

You can enrich the mustache penne with additional seasonal vegetables like asparagus, chopped fresh spinach, peas, prawns or zucchini, bacon or speck.

You can replace tomato sauce with previously browned fresh tomatoes and add them later to the fresh cream.

Tagliatelle al Ragù Bianco (Tagliatelle with White Ragù)

Prep time: 20 minutes

Cook time: 90 minutes

Serves: 4

Difficulty: Easy

Cost: Low

Ingredients:

- 150 g Fresh sausage

- 100 g Bacon

- 250g egg noodles

- 250 g Chopped beef

- 60 g Carrots

- 60 g Celery

- 60 g White wine

- 50 g Extra virgin olive oil

- 1 sprig rosemary

- 60 g Golden onions

- 1 Garlic clove

- 2 Laurel leaves

- 3 Sage leaves

- Water to taste

- Black pepper to taste

- Salt to taste

Preparation:

1. In preparing the tagliatelle with white ragu, begin from the sauté. Heat the oil with garlic clove in a saucepan and allow it to brown. Add the chopped carrots and celery. Also add the chopped onions and then use a spatula to mix.

2. On low heat, leave them to cook for few minutes and meanwhile, browse and use a knife to chop the rosemary and add it to the sauce. Wash and dry the sage and then browse it and chop it finely and add it to the rest of the sauté and lastly use 2 whole bay leaves to flavor.

3. Now cut the bacon into cubes and brown it together with vegetables using a spatula to mix. Now take care of the sausage. Using a small knife, cut the outer casing lengthwise and use your fingers to remove it. Crumble the sausage and add it to the sauce, with the minced meat and over high heat, cook while using a spatula to stir to further break them. Cook for few minutes.

4. Remove the bay leaves and garlic clove and blend with white wine. Continue cooking by adding a ladle of hot water once the wine has evaporated. Use pepper and salt to season and on low heat, cook for about an hour and while adding more water when it's necessary. Turn off the heat after the necessary time.

5. Put a pan on the fire with plenty of water and boil it when at least half an hour is left to the end of cooking. Once it boils, add salt and boil the noodles. Leave them al dente.

6. Drain the pasta al dente and directly transfer it to the saucepan of the meat sauce that is now ready. Mix the pasta very well and then tie the seasoning and adding a little cooking water from the pasta that had been kept aside.

7. Serve your tagliatelle al ragu Bianco while its still steaming.

STORAGE

You can close the tagliatelle with white sauce in an airtight container in the refrigerator for a maximum of 1 day.

Freezing of white meat sauce is possible if fresh ingredients have been used.

ADVICE

You can use pork, rabbit meat, veal or turkey for the white meat sauce.

You can flavor using sausages for example dried porcini mushrooms that are well squeezed and were previously soaked or brawn.

Gnocchi Speck e Noci

(Speck and Walnut Dumplings)

Prep time: 20 minutes

Cook time: 50 minutes

Serves: 4

Difficulty: Medium

Cost: Medium

Ingredients:

Ingredients for the gnocchi:

- 300 g 00 flour

- 1 kg Yellow paste potatoes

- Salt to taste

- 1 Egg

For the dressing:

- 60 g Walnut kernels

- 200 g Speck

- 150 g Fresh liquid cream

- 240 g Taleggio

- Rosemary to taste

- 1 pinch Nutmeg

- Salt to taste

- Black pepper to taste

Preparation:

1. For preparing of potato dumplings, bring the potatoes to boil for 30-40 minutes. Cooking time of the potatoes varies depending of their size.

2. While still hot, peel them and then crush them immediately on the flour that you have poured on the pastry board.

3. Add a pinch of salt and eggs and use your hands to knead until you get compact but soft dough. Take a part of the dough and using your fingertips, roll it out to get 2 com thick loaves. Use semolina to occasionally flour the pastry board. Cut out pieces and drag them on the rigagnocchi to get a typical shape.

4. While you form the potato gnocchi, arrange them well on a tray that is lined with a lightly floured cloth that is well spaced from each other.

5. Now work on the seasoning. Cho the rosemary needles and also cut the taleggio into slices and put them aside. In a large saucepan, pour the fresh cream and use nutmeg to season it. To the cream, add the taleggio and with the help of a whisk, melt it on a low flame.

6. Once the taleggio dissolves, thicken it on the fire so that the sauce isn't too liquid and then remove it from the heat. Cut the speck into medium slices, then reduce it to   strips and then cut them into small cubes.

7. Brown the chopped rosemary with speck and sauté it until it becomes crispy and then keep it aside. Chop the walnuts coarsely and toast them in the same pan with the speck so that they absorb the aroma.

8. In boiling salted water, cook the gnocchi, drain then in the pan with the taleggio sauce as soon as they come to the surface. Add a ladle of water for cooking the gnocchi if necessary and on low flame, mix everything well.

9. Add the walnuts and bacon and if necessary, flavor with black pepper and season with salt.

10. Serve you steaming dumplings and enjoy them.

STORAGE

The walnut and speck dumplings can be kept for few days in the refrigerator.

The potato gnocchi can be kept while still raw. This can be done by leaving them for a couple of hours on the cloth but cooking will be longer in such a case since they will have dried in the air.

Dumplings can be freeze in this way. Put the tray in the freezer and put the potato dumplings in the food bag after 20 minutes and continue until you have frozen all of them. Simply throw them in boiling salted water without defrosting them first to cook them.

ADVICE

You can make an excellent dish should they advance. Empty the fridge, gratinating your advances gnocchi with breadcrumbs that have been flavored with aromatic herbs.

You can enhance this dish with winter scents by adding a mixture of precooked chestnuts.

You can replace the taleggio cheese with any other type of soft cheese like gorgonzola or brie.

Fusilli Panna, Prosciutto e Piselli

(Fusilli with Cream, Ham and Peas)

Prep time: 5 minutes

Cook time: 20 minutes

Serves: 4

Difficulty: Very easy

Cost: Low

Ingredients:

- 320 g Fusilli
- 60 g Golden onions
- 200 g Cooked ham
- 250 g Peas
- 30 g Extra virgin olive oil
- 250 g Fresh liquid cream
- Black pepper to taste
- Salt to taste

Preparation:

1. In making the fusilli with cream, ham and peas, start by putting a pan filled with slightly salted water on the fire for

pasta cooking. Take the cooked ham and first cut it into slices and then into cubes of 1 cm.

2. Chop the onions finely and pour them in a pan where you added the oil. On medium heat, allow them to cook for few minutes and add a ladle of pasta cooking water, peas and on high heat, cook for about 15 minutes.

3. Pour in the cooked ham at this point and sauté them all together for 3 minutes. Add the cream and on low heat, cook for 8 minutes. Meanwhile, cook the pasta and drain it al dente and directly pour it in the dressing.

4. Mix everything well to mix all flavors and serve your fusilli cream and ham while still hot.

STORAGE

You can store your fusilli with cream, ham and peas for a maximum of 1 day in the refrigerator in an airtight container.

ADVICE

You will get the right consistency by cooking the peas for 15 minutes and you will be able to maintain their bright color.

Add a sprinkling of grana to flavor the dish more.

Chapter 3: Fast Sauces

Ricotta and Spinach Ravioli with Butter and Sage

Prep time: 1 hour

Cook time: 10 minutes

Serves: 24

Difficulty: Medium

Cost: Low

Ingredients:

For Ravioli:

- Durum wheat semolina re-milled to taste

- 1 Yolks

- 2 Eggs

- 250 g 00 flour

For Stuffing:

- 50 g Grana Padano DOP to be grated

- 125 g Ricotta

- 250 g Spinach

- Black pepper to taste

- Salt to taste

- Nutmeg to taste

For Dressing:

- 5 leaves Sage

- 40 g Butter

Preparation:

1. Start with the spinach ravioli and the ricotta's fresh egg pasta sheet. Pour flour in a large bowl. Add the yolk and the

eggs. Mix well to combine the ingredients and you use your hands to knead until you get a homogeneous mixture.

2. Move the dough to a working surface that is flour dusted. Vigorously knead the dough until you get dough that is compact and elastic consistent. Mold the dough into a ball and use a plastic wrap to cover it so that it does not dry and allow a minimum of 30 minutes to rest.

3. Meanwhile, fill the ravioli as the pasta is resting. Add the well-rinsed spinach into a non-stick pan. Turn the heat to low and cover with a lid and cook.

4. Cook the spinach for about 7 minutes or until soft. When they are cooked, drain and squeeze them to remove all extra liquids. This will prevent the ravioli dough from being too liquid.

5. In a different bowl, add in the grated cheese and the ricotta. Add spinach and flavor with the nutmeg. Combine the ingredients thoroughly and then move the mixture into a sac-à-poche that is disposable and then set it aside.

6. Remove the plastic wrap from the dough and divide it into two. Use the re-milled semolina flour it lightly and roll one piece of the dough with a machine (the other piece should

remain covered with the plastic wrap). Pass the dough into the rollers of a pasta machine starting from the widest setting to the narrowest until you obtain a sheet that is rectangular in shape with thickness of 2 mm and width of 10 cm. Repeat with the remaining piece of the dough. Place the rolled doughs on a semolina-dusted working surface. Create small filling piles with the sac-à-poche leaving a space of 3 cm between each pile. Use water to brush the sheet edges or you can sprinkle so as to allow adherence of the covering sheet.

7. Lay the next sheet ensuring that the edges fit well. This is so as to prevent ravioli from breaking when cooking, allowing the escape of air between the raviolis. Use your fingers to exert light pressure from the middle of the ravioli. Use a wheel cutter to cut ravioli cubes of 4x4 cm.

8. While creating the ravioli, arrange them on a semolina flour dusted tray and space them to avoid sticking. Add salted water to a pan and bring it to boil. Add the ravioli in when the water starts boiling. As the spinach ravioli and ricotta cook, melt the butter.

9. Chop the sage leaves coarsely and mix. The ravioli that comes on top is ready.

10. Use a slotted spoon to remove them and transfer them straight to the pan for a few minutes. If need be, add some little hot water to prevent the dressing from drying too much.

11. Serve your meal with sage and butter and enjoy.

STORAGE

The ravioli can be store in a refrigerator for up to one day. The ricotta and spinach ravioli can be kept in a freezer for up to a month.

ADVICE

For a crunchy and tasty variant, add a handful of walnut kernels that are finely chopped to the dressing! The resulting dish will be amazingly crunchy.

Spaghetti with Garlic, Oil and Hot Pepper

Prep time: 5 minutes

Cook time: 10 minutes

Serves: 4

Difficulty: Very easy

Cost: Very low

Ingredients:

- 70 g Extra virgin olive oil

- 320 g Spaghetti

- 3 cloves Garlic, peeled

- 3 Fresh chili

Preparation:

1. Bring salted water to boil and cook the pasta. Cook the spaghetti al dente. Meanwhile, get the dressing ready: divide the garlic cloves into half and eliminate the core and slice them thinly.

2. Slice the fresh red pepper by eliminating the stalk. You can remove the seeds if you do not so much spiciness. Add oil into a pan on low heat and add the chili pepper and garlic. Sauté for a few minutes and ensure that that it does not burn.

3. You can tilt the pan to let the oil all over for uniform browning. When the pasta is cooked al dente, move it straight to and pour in a ladle of water.

4. Stir for the flavors to mix and then you can go ahead and serve spaghetti with chili pepper, oil, and garlic.

STORAGE

Eat this recipe while hot. It is not advisable to store.

ADVICE

You can add some chopped parsley if you like.

In White: Butter and Parmesan

Prep time: 5 minutes

Cook time: 10 minutes

Serves: 4

Difficulty: Very easy

Cost: Very low

Ingredients:

- Extra virgin olive oil

- 400 grams of long pasta: linguine, tagliatelle or spaghetti

- 1 clove poached garlic

- Extra virgin olive oil

- Peppercorns to be ground

- 70 grams of Roman pecorino or Parmigiano Reggiano

Preparation:

1. Add 6 tablespoons olive oil in a pan on low heat. Add garlic, pepper and cook for about 5 minutes.

2. In the meantime, bring water to boil and add some salt in it. Add in the pasta and cook al dente. Drain pasta and the get 2 ladles of water and set aside.

3. Add pasta into the frying pan and sauté for some minutes and then eliminate the garlic. Use the parmesan to season and end the cooking by adding a water drop.

4. Add Parmigiano Reggiano, tagliatelle with olive oil, tagliatelle in Bianco and pepper.

5. Serve and use the parmesan and a drizzle of oil to season.

STORAGE

It is recommended that you eat this meal immediately.

ADVICE

Make sure that the pepper is freshly ground every time. The oil gives the pasta a good flavor and it makes it a masterpiece.

Olives in the oil mill, recipe with olive oil, white pasta with oil.

Pasta e Zucchine (Pasta and Courgettes)

Prep time: 5 minutes

Cook time: 15 minutes

Serves: 4

Difficulty: Very easy

Cost: Very low

Ingredients:

- 650 g Zucchini

- 320 g Butterflies

- 20 g Extra virgin olive oil

- Basil to taste

- Salt to taste

- Black pepper to taste

- 1 Garlic clove

Preparation:

1. For preparing the pasta and zucchini, you can start by boiling water in a large saucepan and add some salt once it

boils. In the meantime, wash and dry the courgettes, tick them and use a grater with large holes to grate them.

2. In a large pan, over low heat, pour the extra virgin olive oil and heat it together with a whole garlic clove that has already been peeled. Once the oil is hot, add courgettes that have been seasoned with pepper and salt and cook for 6 minutes occasionally stirring and then remove the garlic.

3. Meanwhile, in boiling and salted water, boil the pasta and drain it al dente and keep aside a little cooking water.

4. Directly pour the pasta into the pan with courgettes together with little cooking water and let it burn for few minutes, mix and then turn off.

5. Use a little chopped basil that you chopped using your hands to perfume everything and now your pasta ad zucchini will be ready to be enjoyed.

STORAGE

You can store your pasta and zucchini in a refrigerator while closed in an airtight container for at least 1 day.

It's not recommended to freeze.

ADVICE

You can indulge yourself and add whatever you like best since pasta and zucchini lends itself to being enriched with many ingredients.

You can grate some grana cheese or salted ricotta if you want and to give an extra flavor to your dish, you cab add smoked bacon or cherry tomatoes.

Chapter 4: Classic Sauces

Tomato and Basil Sauce

Prep time: 10 minutes

Cook time: 30 minutes

Serves: 6

Difficulty: Low

Cost: Low

Ingredients:

- 700 ml Tomato sauce

- 400 g Tomato pulp

- ½ onion

- Salt to taste

- 1 pinch of sugar

- Fresh basil leaves

Preparation:

1. In making the tomato sauce quickly, begin by chopping the golden or the white onion.

2. Put a pot on the oven and put the onions that you chopped and allow then to get soft very well. To avoid darkening, make sure you turn it often.

3. Add the tomato puree and use salt and a pinch of sugar to season it because this helps to reduce the tomato acidity and also add the tomato pulp in small pieces. Allow the sauce to boil over medium heat while its covered.

4. Low the heat once it begins boiling and allow it to cook for 20-25 minutes. Season the sauce with fresh basil leaves that are finely chopped.

5. The tomato sauce is now ready to be used as you like it.

Pesto Sauce

Prep time: 20 minutes

Cook time: 30 minutes

Serves: 2

Difficulty: Easy

Cost: Low

Ingredients:

- 50 ml Extra virgin olive oil

- 15 g Grated Pecorino

- 25 g Basil leaves

- 35 g Parmesan cheese DOP to be grated

- 1 pinch coarse salt.

- 8 g Pine nuts

- ½ Garlic clove

Preparation:

1. In preparing the pesto sauce, make sure you specify that basil leaves shouldn't be washed but you only use a soft

cloth to clean them. You as well ensure that Genoese or Ligurian basil that has leaves that are narrow.

2. To prepare the pesto, put together coarse salt and some peeled garlic in a mortar. Start crushing and once the garlic reduces to cream, add a pinch of coarse salt and basil leaves together and these will help in crushing the fibers better and also help in maintaining the bright and beautiful green color.

3. Against the walls of the mortar, crush the basil by turning the mortar in the opposite direction simultaneously and also turning the pestle from left to right taking it y its ears. Continue doing this until you get a bright and green liquid from the basil leaves. At this particular point, to reduce to cream, add pine nuts and begin beating again.

4. Constantly stir after adding cheese, little at a given time to make the sauce creamier and add extra virgin olive oil as the last one and use a pestle to mix after pouring it flush.

5. Mix all ingredients until you get a homogeneous sauce. The Genoese pesto is now ready for you to use.

STORAGE

You can use an airtight container to store your freshly prepared pesto in a refrigerator and take care and use a layer of oil to cover the sauce. It can be stored for 2-3 days.

You can also use small jars in which you freeze the pesto and then at room temperature of in the refrigerator, defrost it.

ADVICE

Basil also oxidizes just like auberges and apples.

Work on it at the light speed. One of the reasons that cause oxidation is exposure to the oxygen.

Avoid over heating it. You can use a blender if you don't want to see the pestle and mortar and if it's possible, use the plastic blades because metal ones make leaves to become bitter. You will get a delicious and creamier pesto.

You can whisk at the lowest jerky and speed to prevent overheating. For example, you can blend for few seconds, stop it and then start again.

Another trick you can use is to leave the blades and cup in the fridge for at least one hour before.

Cacio and Pepper

Prep time: 10 minutes

Cook time: 10 minutes

Serves: 4

Difficulty: Easy

Cost: Low

Ingredients:

- 200 G Pecorino Romano, medium and to be grated.

- 320 g Spaghetti

- Salt to taste

- Black peppercorns to taste

Preparation:

1. For preparing the spaghetti with pepper and cheese, begin with taking care of grating Pecorino, at least 200 g. In a pan, boil water. For it to be rich in starch, use half of the water than what you always use to cook pasta and add salt to taste once it boils.

2. You can cook the spaghetti once the water is salted. In the meantime, on a cutting board, pour all the peppercorns and use a grinder or meat pestle to mash them. The pungent pepper scent will be more released in such a way.

3. In a large and non-stick pan, pour in half a dose of crushed pepper and over low heat, toast and use a wooden spoon to mix them and then using a couple of ladles of cooking water, blend them.

4. Due to the starch that is contained in water, you will see some bubbles appearing. When they are very al dente, drain the spaghetti and keep aside the cooking water and directly pour into the pan that already has toasted pepper and they will keep cooking with the dressing.

5. Use the kitchen tongs to continuously stir the pasta to make it breathe. To keep cooking by risotto with the spaghetti, add a water ladle or two.

6. Only when more water is needed, continue pouring a water ladle when you realize that the pan is almost completely dry and use the kitchen tongs to stir.

7. Meanwhile, once the pasta is cooked, take care of the Pecorino cream. The cream may get too thick so don't start this operation first.

8. In a bowl, pour in the half dose of grated pecorino and to the grated pecorino, add a ladle of pasta cooking water. Use a whisk to vigorously mix and add more water when needed. Add the remaining pecorino dose and keep a little of it aside to be used for seasoning. Add little more water as it will be needed. In this phase, to get a creamy cream without lumps and that has the right consistency, you may have to calibrate the water dose and the pecorino very well.

9. Finish the pasta cooking and keep adding more hot water when needed. Briefly mix the cream by putting the bowl over the pan stream with hot water and use a whisk to mix before adding the pecorino cream. You do this in order to bring the cream to a temperature that is the same as for the pasta.

10. Turn off the heat of the pan that has spaghetti and pour in the pecorino cream. Use the kitchen tongs to continuously move the spaghetti while pouring the pecorino cream on it. You can as well pour the pecorino that you had kept aside.

11. Mix and then sauté the pasta again and then you can now serve your spaghetti with pepper and cheese and the remaining pepper, season it. Immediately enjoy it in all its creaminess.

STORAGE

It's advisable to immediately consume the spaghetti cacio e pepe.

Conservation of any form is not recommended.

ADVICE

It's crucial to use less pasta cooking water because to determine the phantom cream and also avid lumps, there is one of the most important elements, wetting the pecorino and spaghetti with cooking water that is very rich in starch and hot.

It is advisable to make half a dose if you want to test your cheese and pepper making skills. This is because it makes it easier to manage those cream cheese ingredients.

For short pasta lovers, you can use rigatoni or half sleeves instead of spaghetti.

You can grate some lemon zest in the pecorino cream if you want to slightly degrease the dish.

Arrabbiata Sauce

Prep time: 15 minutes

Cook time: 10 minutes

Serves: 4

Difficulty: Easy

Cost: Very low

Ingredients:

- 380 g Peeled tomatoes, dried
- 3 dry small chilies
- 1 Garlic clove
- Extra virgin olive oil to taste
- Parsley to taste
- 320 g Penne Rigate
- Salt to taste

Preparation:

1. In preparation of Arrabbiata sauce, begin with draining the peeled tomatoes. After that, transfer them in a bowl and use a fork to mash and then chop them.

2. At this given point, use a knife to chop the dried chili and use your hands to crumble it. On the fire, put a pan filled with water add salt to taste and then cook the pasta.

3. In a pan, pour in a generous oil amount and add the chili pepper and peeled garlic clove. Leave then gently and then add tomatoes and then mix everything together then use salt to season. Cook for about 12 minutes while they are covered with a lid and occasionally stir.

4. Cook the pasta al dente by following the cooking times that are shown on the package when the sauce is almost cooked. Remove the lid and remove the garlic after 12 minutes. Drain the pasta and directly transfer it to the sauce.

5. For a moment, skip it and if necessary, add the cooking water. Add chopped parsley and mix for one more and last time and then you can serve your sauce.

STORAGE

It's advisable to consume the Arrabbiata sauce while it is still fresh. As an alternative, you can keep in the refrigerator for 1 day.

ADVICE

Garnish each dish using pecorino Romana and also use fresh chili.

Puttanesca Sauce

Prep time: 20 minutes

Cook time: 20 minutes

Serves: 4

Difficulty: Easy

Cost: Low

Ingredients:

- 10 g Capers in salt

- 800 g Peeled tomatoes

- 3 Garlic cloves

- 1 bunch Parsley to be minced

- 30 g Extra virgin olive oil

- 320 g Spaghetti

- 25 g Anchovies in oil

- 2 Dry chilies

- 100 g Gaeta olives

- Salt to taste

Preparation:

1. To make the puttanesca sauce, begin with rinsing the capers under running water in order to remove the excess salt. Dry them and put them on a cutting board to coarsely chop them.

2. Use the knife blade to mash the pitted Gaeta olives. Also wash the parsley, dry it and then mince it.

3. On the fire, put a full pot of water and bring it to boil, once it boils, add salt. This water will be used for pasta cooking.

4. In a large pan, pour the chopped dried chilies, peeled and left garlic cloves and oil. Add the desalted capers and anchovy fillets.

5. Over medium heat, brown them for at least 5 minutes while you are stirring occasionally so that the anchovies release all the aromas after melting.

6. Pour the lightly crushed and peeled tomatoes at this point and use a spoon to mix and then over medium heat, cook them for another 10 minutes. In the meantime, boil the spaghetti al dente.

7. Remove the garlic cloves and add the crushed olives once the sauce is ready. Use chopped fresh parsley to flavor the sauce.

8. Meanwhile bring the pasta to cooking and then directly drain it in a pan and then sauté for half a minute. This time is enough to mix all flavors.

9. You may now serve the puttanesca sauce still hot.

STORAGE

It's not recommended to freeze.

It's advisable to immediately consume the spaghetti puttanesca. You can cover them using a plastic wrap and keep them in the refrigerator for 1 day if they advance.

ADVICE

You can make a fresh and good sauce when the tomatoes are in season.

We recommend you to avoid adding more salt since this dish is very savory.

Spaghetti with Tomato Sauce

Prep time: 20 minutes

Cook time: 80 minutes

Serves: 4

Difficulty: Very easy

Cost: Very low

Ingredients:

- 4 basil leaves

- 1 clove, garlic

- Salt

- 800 g peeled tomatoes

- 30 g extra virgin olive oil

- 320 g spaghetti

Preparation:

To prepare the spaghetti with tomato sauce, you start with preparing the sauce.

1. Pour the peeled garlic clove, divide it in half to remove the soul and make the perfume delicate, and extra virgin olive oil.

2. Over a high flame, cook for 2 minutes. Then add the peeled tomatoes and salt. On very low heat, cook for like 1 hour and let the sauce gently simmer.

3. Occasionally stir and when the indicated time is over, remove the garlic. Pass the tomatoes in a vegetable mill so as to get a homogeneous and smooth puree.

4. Turn on very low heat and transfer the sauce back to the pan and add basil leaves. Turn off the sauce after few minutes and keep it warm. Cook the pasta in much boiling salted water and then directly dry in into the sauce.

5. Stir for few seconds, open the flame and constantly stir to mix everything well. Your spaghetti with tomatoes is ready.

6. Serve and garnish with fresh basil leaves.

STORAGE

Prepare the sauce with little advance or refrigerate for 2-3 days as long as it's covered well in a hermetically resealable glass container or a plastic wrap. You can also freeze the sauce if you want.

ADVICE

The longer you cook the tomato, the tastier flavor guaranteed. Add a little tomato paste for a more intense color.

Piccadilly gives more sweetness to the sauce and you can as well use San Marzano tomatoes.

Norma Sauce

Prep time: 20 minutes

Cook time: 1 hour

Serves: 4

Difficulty: Easy

Cost: Low

Ingredients:

- 1 wire Extra virgin olive oil

- 200 g Salted ricotta

- 320 g Striped celery

- 500 g Eggplants

- 850 g Auburn tomatoes

- 10 g Fresh basil

- 2 garlic cloves

- Salt to taste

For frying

- Extra virgin olive oil to taste

Preparation:

1. In preparing the pasta alla Norma, take the auburn tomatoes and rinse them. Cut them into quarters after drying them.

2. Pour a drizzle of oil in a deep-bottomed pan and fry 2 clean and whole garlic cloves but you can as well remove them if you want.

3. Once the garlic suffers for few moments, pour in the tomatoes and over low heat, cook while they are covered using a lid for about 20 minutes until the tomatoes have released the sauce and are soft.

4. Transfer them to a vegetable mill put on a bowl once they are ready and in order to get a smooth and juicy pulp, pass them.

5. Transfer everything back to the pan and then salt them. Cook until they shrink for about 10-15 minutes. Then get a

pan and fill it with water, then boil it, add salt once it has boiled.

6. In the meantime, wash the auberges dry and tick them and cut them in slices of 9 mm. There is no need of purging the aubergines of you use the ones commonly on the market unless you know that the ones you are using are bitter.

7. Use much extra virgin olive oil heated at a temperature of 170 degrees and fry the aubergines. Don't exceed the temperature but keep it constant by frying few aubergines at a time and then go check with a kitchen thermometer.

8. Use a slotted spoon to drain them once they turn golden brown and transfer them to a fried paper sheet to absorb the excess oil. You can then salt them to your taste.

9. Cook the pasta al dente and pour the basil leaves in the sauce with heat off once almost ready. In a pan, stir and directly add the drained pasta. Mix them well to flavor.

10. You can now transfer the pasta to serving dishes and season each portion with abundant fried aubergine slices and with the coarse grater, sprinkle with salted ricotta.

11. You can serve your pasta alla Norma with few aubergine slices. Put them in the center of the serving table so that diners can add as needed.

STORAGE

It's not recommended to freeze.

It's advisable to consume the pasta alla Norma immediately.

ADVICE

Before passing the tomatoes, you can remove the garlic cloves.

If you prefer, add the aubergines to the ready-made sauce but this depends on the pasta alla Norma version you are fond of.

Pasta that is indicated for this kind of preparation is the short one like the half sleeves or rigatoni and stripes celery.

4 Cheeses Sauce

Prep time: 10 minutes

Cook time: 15 minutes

Serves: 4

Difficulty: Easy

Cost: Medium

Ingredients:

- 80 g PDO Parmigiano Reggiano

- 100 g Sweet gorgonzola

- 80 g Soft Taleggio

- 320 g Pennette Rigate

- 1 pinch White pepper

- 180 g Whole milk

- 80 g Grated Gruyere

- Salt to taste

Preparation:

1. In making the 4-cheese pasta, begin by throwing the Pennette Rigate in a pan with boiling salted water immediately.

2. Go to the cheese. Using a mesh grater, grate the gruyere cheese and pass the taleggio cheese through cutting it in small cubes and lastly remove the crust from the gorgonzola and cut it in small pieces.

3. On the stove, put a saucepan and pour milk inside and on low heat, let it heat for few minutes. Then add the taleggio and gorgonzola. Gently stir to help in melting and lastly add the grated parmesan and the gruyere.

4. For few moments, continue stirring and then turn off the flame. The pasta should be cooked at this point. Use a slotted spoon to drain it, part of the water may end up in a pot and then dip it in the cheese cream.

5. Adjusting to the cheese flavor, add pepper and salt. Again, stir and then let it to rest for few moments before you serve.

6. Your pasta with 4 cheeses is now ready. Taste it while still creamy and hot.

STORAGE

It is good to consume the 4-cheese pasta immediately once it is ready. Actually, the cheese tends to thicken with cooling and resting and transforming everything to a large block.

You can prepare the cheese sauce in advance and keep it well covered in a refrigerator for at least up to 2 days.

To restore its velvety consistency, melt it in a pot with a little milk or in a water bath.

ADVICE

Remember to keep a certain balance between aged or spicy cheeses and more delicate ones.

For a pleasant meeting, add terracotta cubes.

Grilled slices or vegetables with sautéed cubes are best if you want to stay in the vegetarian guise.

Pasta and Beans

Prep time: 15 minutes

Cook time: 110 minutes

Serves: 4

Difficulty: Very easy

Cost: Low

Ingredients:

- 320 g Ditaloni Rigate
- 250 g Tomato sauce
- 200 g Dried borlotti beans
- 80 g Raw ham
- 30 g Celery
- 80 g Lard
- 30 g Onions
- 1 Garlic clove
- 2 Laurel leaves
- 10 g Extra virgin olive oil
- 30 g Carrots
- 3 Rosemary sprigs
- Black pepper to taste

- Salt to taste

Preparation:

1. In preparing pasta and beans, begin with soaking the beans overnight. The following day, rinse them and transfer them to a pot. Use plenty of water to cover them, add 2 bay leaves and then boil them for the next 80 minutes.

2. In the meantime, prepare other recipe ingredients. Finely chop the celery, carrots and onions after cleaning them and cut the lard into strips and the ham too.

3. In a saucepan, heat the oil, add the chopped vegetables and peeled garlic cloves and fry them for 5 minutes. Add lard and ham strips and cook again for some minutes. Use a slotted spoon to take the beans and add then to sauté and then add a ladle of the cooking water.

4. Keep the remaining cooking water because you may need to use it later. In a pot, pour in the salt in moderation, pepper and tomato puree and on moderate flame, cook them for 20 minutes and you can add the pasta after that.

5. From the mixture, take two ladles and put them into a container and use an immersion blender to blend them before adding the pasta and then set the cream aside.

6. Directly to the pan, add the ditaloni Rigate and cover using the cooking water from the beans and on moderate flame, cook the pasta and keep stir occasionally.

7. Add the chopped rosemary and   the previously blended mixture when the pasta is al dente and then turn off the heat. Use a lid to cover and allow it to rest for 3 minutes.

8. Your pasta and beans are ready to be served after your last sprinkling of black pepper.

STORAGE

Pasta and beans can be kept in an airtight container for one day in a refrigerator.

Freezing is not advisable.

You can keep the bean dressing without pasta in a refrigerator for 2-3 days.

ADVICE

For your pasta with beans to be more genuine and good, finish it with a pinch of chili pepper and drizzle of raw oil.

For a more delicate taste or indulging in pasta shapes, you can replace borlotti beans with cannellini beans upon preference.

Porcini Mushrooms Sauce

Prep time: 50 minutes

Cook time: 15 minutes

Serves: 4

Difficulty: Medium

Cost: Medium

Ingredients:

Ingredients for fresh pasta

- Semolina to sprinkle to taste

- 120 g Fresh eggs

- 200 g 00 flour

To season

- 50 g Butter

- 500 g Porcini mushrooms

- Salt to taste

- 1 Garlic clove

- 1 Parsley sprig

- 35 g Extra virgin olive oil

- Black pepper to taste

Preparation:

1. In preparation of Porcini mushrooms sauce, begin with the fresh pasta. In a bowl or pastry board, pour the flour, form a classic fountain shape and in the center, pour in the previously beaten eggs.

2. To get consistent dough that is not too dry or too sticky, it is advisable to respect the recommended egg doses. Using a fork, start mixing from the center and collect the flour gradually. Work with your hands and vigorously knead when the dough is more compact. Do this for about 10 minutes.

3. Give a spherical shape to the dough and use a cling film to wrap it and allow it to rest away from heat sources in a cool place at room temperature for 30 minutes.

4. In the meantime, concentrate on the porcini mushrooms. Using a small knife, scrap the stem and clean them from the soil. You can use a slightly dampened cloth to clean them if

they are very dirty. You can as well pass them under cold running water quickly and then use a cloth to dry them perfectly. Mushrooms absorb too much water and so may lose their consistency and flavor so if you decide to use this option, do it so quickly and then cut them in slices.

5. On very low heat, pour the butter in a large saucepan and pour in the oil when the butter is almost melted completely. Allow it to slightly warm up and then pour in 1 whole garlic clove, you can chop it if you want and the porcini mushrooms.

6. Add pepper and salt to your taste and then cook the mushrooms for a period of 10 minutes. You can remove the whole garlic if you had added it after the cooking and once it is ready, keep it warm. Finely chop the parsley and set it aside.

7. Take the dough and divide it in 16 pieces after the necessary resting time. For the piece to be passed in the machine to be rolled, flour it lightly. Cover the remaining dough with a plastic wrap and keep it aside.

8. Passing from the largest to the penultimate thickness, insert the first piece into the machine and keep the remaining dough aside. Use a plastic wrap to cover it.

9. Once you reach to the penultimate step of the machine, Go again over the dough strip. To pull the dough well, two steps at this thickness will be required.

10. Use semolina flour to lightly flour the work surface and roll out the first sheet. Continue with the rest of the dough pieces until you make various sheets and sprinkle the sheets with semolina and allow them to dry for 5 minutes in order to finish the dough.

11. Of each sheet, fold the shorter side inwards and then roll the dough on itself. Begin making the tagliatelle by cutting to a 6.5-7 mm thickness using a lightly floured and sharp knife.

12. To make the nests of noodles, lift every roll and place them gradually on a tray or a work surface part that has been lightly floured with semolina flour.

13. Boil the water then add salt. Cook the noodles for 3-4 minutes. Directly drain into the seasoning. Keep the cooking water. On low heat, add the seasonings and ingredients in a pan and mix them together. Add the chopped parsley and to prevent the noodles from becoming too dry, you can add a ladle of pasta cooking water.

14. Now your noodles with porcini mushrooms are now ready. Serve and enjoy.

STORAGE

Keep the noodles in a fridge for at least 1 day. You can as well eat them immediately.

You can alternatively freeze them raw. To do so, on the tray, put the well-spaced pasta nests and then put then in a freezer for a couple of hours to harden. Once well-hardened, put them in frost bags, it's better if they are already portioned and take them back to the freezer. In case you need to use them, directly boil them from frozen in boiling water and then proceed per the recipe.

ADVICE

You can give an extra freshness note and particularly with fresh mint instead of parsley.

To make the perfect tagliatelle, wet the dough with little water that is at room temperature if the dough is too dry during the processing time since the dough absorbs too many liquids.

On the contrary if it turns out to be too sticky, without exaggerating, add a little flour. It is advised to always use a high-quality flour and fresh eggs in the weight indicated.

Trofie alla Portofino

Prep time: 30 minutes

Cook: 30 minutes

Serves: 4

Difficulty: very easy

Cost: Low

Ingredients:

- 250 g Cherry tomatoes, washed and cut into half

- 350 g Trofie

- ¼ tsp Salt

- Extra virgin olive oil

For The Pesto

- 35 g Parmesan cheese, grated

- 50 ml Extra virgin olive oil

- 25 g Basil

- 1 clove Garlic

- 15 g Pecorino, Grated

- 7 g Pine nuts

- 1 pinch Coarse sea salt

Preparation:

1. In making Portofino, you prepare pesto by following Genoese Pesto recipe. Add garlic in a mortar and crush it. Add salt and basil leaves and crush the basil by moving the pestle from right to left while moving the mortar from left to right (opposite direction). Add pine nuts and crush them again. Add cheese and extra virgin olive oil. Keep mixing to form homogeneous sauce. Your pesto is now ready. Set aside.

2. Add olive oil to a pan on medium heat. Add the tomatoes and season with salt. Cook until tomatoes are ready.

3. Add tomatoes to a vegetable mill and remove the seeds by sieving them. When done, add the sieved tomatoes to a pan.

4. Add pesto and stir to combine until a homogeneous sauce is formed. Lastly make the trofie: bring salted water to boil in a pan on medium heat and add trofie.

5. Cook the trofie and when ready, drain and add tomato sauce and pesto. Mix and then serve.

STORAGE

Store the Portofino trofie in a fridge in a container that is air-tight for a few of days.

For the Portofino trofie, it's not advisable to freeze. As for the sauce, it can be prepared earlier and put in a freezer.

ADVICE

Use basil leaves to decorate the Portofino trofie dish as it adds to the flavor.

Pici all'Aglione

Prep time: 15 minutes

Cook time: 30 minutes

Serves: 4

Difficulty: Easy

Cost: Low

Ingredients:

- 5 tbsps. Extra virgin olive oil
- 6 garlic cloves
- 700 g Auburn tomatoes
- 1 chili, fresh
- 1 tbsp white wine vinegar
- 360 g Pici
- Salt

Preparation:

1. To prepare the pici all'aglione Blanch the tomatoes in boiling water for 1 minute. Remove the seeds after peeling and cut them into small cubes.

2. Using the blade of a thick knife, crush the garlic after cutting it into slices.

3. Get a pan and put cooking oil, add the chili pepper finely chopped and seeded and crushed garlic, on very low heat, brown it. The garlic must only melt, it shouldn't darken and the sauté should cook slowly.

4. Leave the garlic on the fire for like 10 minutes until it starts to melt. Add the chopped tomatoes and vinegar as well and season with salt. Over medium low heat, cook the tomatoes for about 20 minutes until they make a creamy sauce.

5. Meanwhile, put the salted water to boil. This water is for the pasta. If the sauce excessively dries out, add like 2/3 ladles of pasta cooking water.

6. Dip the pici when the water has boiled and after cooking for like 18 minutes, drain them and transfer them in the sauce for flavoring.

7. Serve the pici all'aglione while hot.

STORAGE

It is not recommended to prepare the pici all'aglione in advance or freeze them. Eat it on the spot once its cooked.

ADVICE

Avoid blanching the tomatoes before peeling them especially if they are very ripe. Pici can also be tried with an excellent ragu.

Pasta e Patate (Pasta and Potatoes)

Prep time: 15 minutes

Cook time: 30 minutes

Serves: 4

Difficulty: Very easy

Cost: Very low

Ingredients:

- 700 g Yellow- fleshed potatoes

- Thyme to taste

- 30 g Extra virgin olive oil

- 250 g Pipe Rigate

- Salt to taste

- 40 g Shallot

- Black pepper to taste

- Rosemary to taste

Preparation:

1. In preparing pasta and potatoes, begin with peeling the potatoes and then thoroughly wash and dry them using a clean cloth and cut them into cubes.

2. Clean and also chop the shallot finely and also chop the rosemary. Boil plenty of water in a pot and salt it once it boils. This water will be sued to boil the pasta and also lengthen the seasoning.

3. In a large pan, heat the extra virgin olive oil and then add the chopped shallot rosemary and the shallot and allow it to brown for few minutes and make sure you don't burn them.

4. You can now add the cubed potatoes and cook them while stirring often and when necessary adding a ladle of boiling water at a time. This will take like 20 minutes.

5. Use pepper and salt to season once the potatoes are once cooked. Meanwhile the water for cooking the pasta will have also boiled and then you cook and then directly drain al dente into the pan with potatoes and mix well and finish the cooking by adding a little cooking water from the pasta when needed. You will create a delicious creamy sauce by

combining potatoes and pasta in the same pan. Thanks to the starch which is released by the potatoes and the pasta.

6. Lastly, use few thyme leaves and pepper to season and then turn off the heat. Use a drizzle of raw extra virgin olive oil to season.

7. You can now serve your pasta and potatoes while still hot and enjoy.

STORAGE

You can keep your potatoes and pasta for a maximum of 1 day closed in an airtight container in a refrigerator. It is not recommended to freeze.

ADVICE

You can choose whether to make the pasta and potatoes dry or rather make them soupy by adding less or more cooking water during the preparation according to your tastes.

Pasta Gorgonzola e Noci (Gorgonzola and Walnut Pasta)

Prep time: 10 minutes

Cook time: 15 minutes

Serves: 4

Difficulty: Very easy

Cost: Low

Ingredients:

- 320 g Trofie

- 150 g Fresh liquid cream

- Thyme to taste

- 350 g Sweet gorgonzola

- Black pepper to taste

- 100 g Walnut kernels

- Salt to taste

Preparation:

1. For preparation of gorgonzola pasta and walnuts, begin by putting a pan with water for pasta cooking on the fire. Add salt once it comes to boil.

2. On the cutting board, use a knife to chop the walnut kernels and set them aside. Now switch to gorgonzola. Slice and then remove the rind and cut them into cubes.

3. In a large saucepan, pour in the fresh liquid cream and heat for 2-3 minutes and then pour in the gorgonzola cubes. Add a few thyme leaves and a pinch of ground black pepper and cook for 2-3 minutes over medium heat.

4. Meanwhile, through the pasta in boiling water and as soon as it is cooked al dente and drain it al dente. Directly dip the trofie into the dressing and stir to mix everything well.

5. Lastly add the chopped walnuts and mix it one more time. Your gorgonzola and walnuts pasta are now ready. Serve it immediately.

STORAGE

It is recommended to immediately consume the dish. You can keep the gorgonzola pasta and walnuts for a maximum of 1 day in the refrigerator if you prefer keeping them and heat then when necessary.

ADVICE

Use grated cheese such as pecorino or parmesan to strengthen the flavor of the gorgonzola and walnut paste.

Pasta agli Asparagi (Pasta with Asparagus)

Prep time: 20 minutes

Cook time: 20 minutes

Serves: 4

Difficulty: Easy

Cost: Low

Ingredients:

- 700 g Fresh asparagus

- 20 g Parmesan cheese DOP to be grated

- 320 g Penne Rigate

- 80 g Shallot

- 3 g Thyme

- Black pepper to taste

- Salt to taste

Preparation:

1. Begin by putting a pan on the fire with plenty of hot water. Add salt when it boils. This water will be used in cooking the pasta.

2. Now go to asparagus cleaning. Under plenty of running water, wash them and use a cloth to dry them. By drawing them deprive them of the harder and light-colored ends.

3. Using a potato peeler, remove the outer part of the stem, the leatherier one. Take the asparagus and align them in a bunch and taking care to leave the tips intact. Cut the stalks into small rounds.

4. Finely chop the shallot at this point. Continue to take a non-stick pan. Pour on it a drizzle of oil and fry the shallot gently. Occasionally stir and add a ladle of cooking water to dry it more gently without the risk of the burning.

5. Add the tips and the chopped asparagus, pepper and salt. Mix and then pour in one or two hot water ladles and cover with a lid and over moderate heat, cook for 10-15 minutes.

6. In the pot of boiling water, boil the pasta while the asparagus is cooking and with the help of a slotted spoon,

transfer it to the pan where you cooked the asparagus once its al dente and then mix.

7. Lastly, use grated parmesan and thyme leaves to flavor and wet with a little cooking water if its necessary and turn off the heat after stirring.

8. Serve your pasta with asparagus and enjoy the meal.

STORAGE

It's recommended to consume the freshly cooked asparagus pasta. If some is left over, put it in a tightly closed container and keep it in the refrigerator for a maximum of 2 days.

Freezing is not recommended.

ADVICE

Do you want an original variant of this dish? Using a mixer, just blend the parmesan, asparagus and thyme and create an appetizing and thick cream that will be used to season this delicious asparagus pasta.

Pasta e Piselli (Pasta with Green Peas)

Prep time: 20 minutes

Cook time: 30 minutes

Serves: 4

Difficulty: Very easy

Cost: Very low

Ingredients:

- 320 g Ditaloni Rigate

- 100 g Fresh spring onions

- 1 kg Peas fresh whole Shelling

- 30 g Extra virgin olive oil

- Black pepper to taste

- 30 g Grated Parmigiano Reggiano DOP

- Salt to taste

Preparation:

1. In making the pasta and peas, boil water in a large pan and once it boils, salt it and keep it for pasta cooking. In the

meantime, shell the peas in a bowl and collect them. Take the spring onion and remove the base. Divide it in half lengthwise and slice each half. It will be more practical to cut it in this way.

2. In the pan, pour the olive oil and the freshly sliced spring onion that ahs been wet with a pasta ladle cooking water and allow it to stew until it is soft or for 15 minutes. Add more cooking water if it should dry out too much.

3. Add the pepper, salt, shelled fresh peas and another ladle of cooking water once the onion is stewed and cook for at least 10 minutes.

4. Now for only 5 minutes, boil the pasta because then it will finish cooking in the pan with peas. For flavoring it more use risottarla. Use a slotted spoon to drain the pasta directly into the pan with peas. Cook the pasta and adding the cooking water gradually and before adding more, take care to wait till the liquid is well absorbed. This will take like 5 minutes.

5. Season with grated parmigiano Reggiano once cooked. Mix to flavor and add pepper and salt to taste. Your pasta and peas are now ready. Serve them hot.

STORAGE

You can store the pasta and peas in a closed refrigerator in an airtight container for at most 1 day. If you have used fresh peas, you can freeze them once cooked. However, it is not recommended to freeze the pasta and peas.

ADVICE

Do you desire adding an aromatic note to your pasta and peas?

To those who don't give up fragrant herbs, a sprinkle of nutmeg for spice lovers with few thyme leaves is a perfect solution.

Fettuccine al Tartufo (Fettuccine with Truffle)

Prep time: 15 minutes

Cook time: 15 minutes

Serves: 4

Difficulty: Easy

Cost: High

Ingredients:

- 1 Garlic clove

- 80 g Black truffle

- 250 g Egg Fettuccine

- 40 g Butter

- 50 g Extra virgin olive oil

- Salt to taste

Preparation:

1. In preparation of fettuccine with truffle, begin by cleaning the truffle. Under the jet of cold water, thoroughly rinse to

remove the excess oil then use a semi-hard brush or just a brush to brush it to remove any trace of impurities and carefully dry it before putting it on the cutting board to slice.

2. Using the special truffle cutter, slice the truffle into very thin strips and keep them aside. In a pan on low heat, heat the oil and melt the butter.

3. Clean the garlic clove by removing the internal sprout and allow it to brown in the pan with melted butter and oil for few minutes. Use a fork to remove it and turn off the heat and then add the previously sliced truffle flakes. You can keep some aside for the final decoration of the dish.

4. With the heat off, let the seasoning season and mixing the truffle flakes gently and in the meantime, you can cook the egg fettuccine in much salted water.

5. Dip them in the truffle-based dressing after draining them al dente and thoroughly mix and add the cooking water of the pasta to bind if necessary.

6. Your dish is now ready. Serve it with plenty of black truffle flakes.

STORAGE

Truffle is a delicate ingredient. You can keep it in a cool place for a short period, a maximum of 8 days when closed in a glass jar and wrapped in a breathable gauze.

ADVICE

Make sure to clean the truffle well from all traces of soil before tasting it. You can clean it by moderately rinsing it or brushing it using a brush with semi-hard bristles.

Chapter 5: Fish Sauces

Clam Sauce

Prep time: 20 minutes

Cook time: 20 minutes

Serves: 4

Difficulty: Easy

Cost: Medium

Ingredients:

- 1 bunch Parsley

- 1 kg Clams

- 320 g Spaghetti

- 1 clove Garlic

- Coarse salt for clams to taste

- Salt to taste

- Black pepper to taste

- Extra virgin olive oil to taste

Preparation:

1. Clean the spaghetti and discard any broken shells. Break them on a cutting board or beat them against a sink. This helps in checking if there is sand present inside; the bivalves without sand will be closed while the ones with sand will open. Put a colander in a bowl and place the clams inside to rinse them. Put colander in a bowl and sprinkle with lots of salt. Let the clams soak for about two and half hours.

2. After that tie, any residual sand will be purged. Heat oil in saucepan under medium heat and add garlic. Carefully

drain the clams, rinse and immerse them in the pan. Cover and cook on high heat for several minutes.

3. When heated, the clams will open. Occasionally shake the pan as you cook until they open fully. Turn the heat off when they all open. Drain the bivalves and collect the juice. Meanwhile, add the spaghetti to boiling salted water and when you are halfway through, drain them.

4. Pour sauce into a pan. Pour the spaghetti in too and go on cooking. When done with cooking, add chopped parsley and the clams and blast once and your meal is ready.

5. Serve and enjoy immediately.

STORAGE

You can store freshly made spaghetti for up to a day in the fridge but ensure that it is put in an airtight container. For the clams, put them in a bowl wrapped with a damp cloth or full of cold water

ADVICE

Use excellent clams so that the freshness and the taste of the product can be savored. Add more tomatoes if want color.

Tuna Sauce

Prep time: 5 minutes

Cook time: 10 minutes

Serves: 4

Difficulty: Very easy

Cost: Very low

Ingredients:

- 400 g Peeled tomatoes

- 150 g Tuna in oil, drained

- 320 g Spaghetti

- ½ Golden onion

- Black pepper to taste

- Extra virgin olive oil to taste

- Salt to taste

- Basil to taste

Preparation:

1. Start by bringing salted water to boil. You will use this water in cooking pasta. Meanwhile peel and chop the onion thinly. Add olive oil to a pan and fry the onion. Sauté for a few minutes while stirring until onions are dry.

2. Use your hands to fray the tuna and put it on the pan. Sauté for some minutes until it is brown as you stir occasionally. Use a fork to mash the tomatoes and then add to the pan. Cook for about 9-11 minutes.

3. At the meantime, boil the spaghetti and cook al dente. As the pasta cooks, the sauce will be ready. Drain straight into tuna pan.

4. Use pepper to season and then turn the heat off. Add basil leaves and mix the spaghetti and tuna and serve.

STORAGE

For storage of tuna spaghetti, put them in an airtight container and place in a fridge for up to a day.

ADVICE

If you want a blank version, add oil in a pan and sauté the tuna and the onion for about 4 minutes. Add spaghetti al dente, sauté and add parsley.

Marinara Sauce

Prep time: 20 minutes

Cook time: 20 minutes

Serves: 4

Difficulty: Medium

Cost: Very high

Ingredients:

- 320 g Half paccheri

- 4 Scallops with shell

- 500 g Tomato sauce

- 190 g, Shrimp

- 1 glass Water

- 300 g Datterini tomatoes

- 340 g Scampi

- 4 King prawns

- 1 clove Garlic

- Parsley to taste

- Dried chili to taste

- Basil to taste

- Salt to taste

- Extra virgin olive oil to taste

To cook mussels and clams

- 740 g Clams

- 680 g Mussels

- 1 clove Garlic

- Extra virgin olive oil to taste

Preparation:

1. To make marinara pasta, start by cleaning the seafood. Ensure that there aren't any empty or broken shells: discard any that you find present. Take the seafood to a cutting board to remove any sand present. Place a colander in a bowl and put clams in it to rinse.

2. Move colander to a water-filled bowl and add salt and soak for about two and half hours. Any residual sand present will be purged by the clams will purge.

3. In the meantime, clean the mussels. Use running water to wash them. Remove all the incrustations using a small knife and remove the beard manually with an energetic movement. Rub the mussels vigorously under running water to remove impurities that could be present.

4. Work on scallops. Remove the scallops from shells and set them aside. They will decorate. Remove coral and place them aside.

5. Get the prawns, remove the carapace and leave only the head and cut the slightly at the back. Remove the intestine.

6. Clean the pink prawns by leaving the head and eliminating the carapace. Put them on a chopping board and cut into half the body and the head.

7. Widen the head and leave the tail section closed. This will give the sauce more flavor and also get rid of earthy filament.

To Prepare the Pasta

1. Add oil in a saucepan with high edges. Chop the garlic clove and add it in. allow about 2 minutes for it to brown. Add clams and mussels.

2. Use a lid to cover and let them heat. Use a twist to turn them without uncovering the lid. By turning them the ones at the bottom will come up. When they all open, uncover and use a slotted spoon to mix. Avoid overcooking, as they will dry. Drain using a skimmer and then move the clams and the mussels to a platter. Leave the sauce.

3. Get rid of the garlic. Get about half of the mussels and half of clams and clean them, separating the shells from the fruits. The rest will be for plate decorating. Given the clams are cleaned, there will be residue at the pan's base. In a small bowl, place a colander carefully and the filter the sauce. Watch out so that you don't spill it at the base off the pan.

4. You now will have got cooking water of clams and mussels. Add oil in a pan and add the garlic in. sauté it for about 2 minutes until it is brown. Remove from heat. Blend the garlic with cooking water of clams and mussels, add in small amounts watching not get yourself burnt.

5. Put the pan on heat and pour in one glass of water and let it boil for about 5 minutes. Add in tomato puree. Add water into the bowl with the tomato to recover any remaining tomato and add it to the pot.

6. Cook for about 11 minutes. Meanwhile, add half paccheri to salted boiling water to cook it. Ensure that you consistently stir to avoid sticking. Cook for about 20 minutes. Meanwhile, cut the cherry tomatoes into two. Add the scallops and prawns after 12 minutes of cooking. Arrange them nicely to get the sauce flavored. Put prawns as a lid on the scallop shells.

7. Increase the heat a little and then pour in the clams and mussels that were unshelled. You can add one ladle of pasta cooking water if the sauce has shrunk.

8. Pour in the cherry tomatoes and cook for about 3-4 minutes and lower the heat. Transfer the prawns and the shells to a plate. Drain pasta and add it to the sauce-containing pan.

9. After a few minutes sprinkle some oil and then use a skimmer to move the pasta to a tray. At the top, set the seafood.

10. Boil the sauce that remained and pour it on the pasta. Chop the parsley and basil quickly and add it in the pasta. Add the chili pepper too. Use oil to garnish. Put scallop shells and scampi.

11. Serve and enjoy

STORAGE

You should eat the marinara pasta immediately. Do not store.

ADVICE

The pasta should be hot when serving; you should therefore serve fast.

Maltagliati al Ragu di Seppia

(Maltagliati with Cuttlefish Ragout)

Prep time: 1 hour

Cook time: 35 minutes

Serves: 4

Difficulty: Easy

Cost: Medium

Ingredients:

For Maltagliati

- 300 g 00 flour
- 3 eggs, medium

For the cuttlefish ragout

- 400 g Peeled tomatoes
- 1 onion, small

  3 Thyme sprigs
- 50 ml Dry white wine
- 500 g Cuttlefish, clean
- 2 garlic cloves
- 4 fillets, Anchovies in oil
- 2 tbsps. Parsley, chopped

283

- 3 tbsps. Extra virgin olive oil
- Black pepper and salt

Preparation:

1. Making the Maltagliati with cuttlefish ragout, begin by preparing the fresh egg pasta. I a large bowl, put the sifter flour, insert the three shelled eggs in a hole you have made in the center, then break the eggs, knead with your hands and put together all the ingredients.

2. On a floured surface, turn the dough upside down and work until it becomes homogeneous and smooth. You can add a drop of water if the dough is too dry. Wrap the dough in a cling film and let it rest in a cool place that is free from drafts but not in a refrigerator so that it can be spread better for at least an hour.

3. Meanwhile as the egg pasta rests, detach the tentacles from the body of the cuttlefish and set aside. Cut the cuttlefish bags into strips and them into small cubes. Keep aside the anchovy fillets after cutting them into small pieces.

4. In a pan with olive oil and on low heat, chop the small onions and cook them and the crushed garlic cloves as well. Also add the chopped anchovies and melt them over low heat. Lastly add the thyme leaves. To a pan, add the

cuttlefish tentacles and the cubes and fry them till brown for few minutes.

5. To the white wine, add the cuttlefish and once it evaporates fully which process will take like 10 minutes, add the peeled tomatoes. Season them with pepper and salt and cook until the cuttlefish is tender and the tomato has shrunk. Before turning off the heat, add the chopped parsley.

6. Roll the egg pasta on a floured surface using a machine or a rolling pin to roll out the dough in a sheet about 1 mm think that you will flour nicely. Use a knife to cut the dough into regular strips.

7. After dividing the strips of pasta obtained in half, overlap them and cut them into irregular lozenges. Spread the Maltagliati on a pastry board of floured cloth without overlapping them. In a large saucepan, boil the Maltagliati in boiling salted water cook them and leave them al dente then.

8. Drain and then pour then into a pan directly with the cuttlefish ragout. Use a wooden spoon and mix well while you sauté for at least 1 minute until your Maltagliati with cuttlefish ragout are ready.

9. You can as well sprinkle ith fresh parsley before putting them on the plate.

STORAGE

You can cover the Maltagliati with cuttlefish ragout with a plastic wrap in a refrigerator for a couple of days.

Ragu can be prepared the day before and kept in a covered refrigerator.

Maltagliati can also be frozen raw. For freezing, put the tray with the Maltagliati in a freezer to harden for some hours. Put them in frost bags when they are well hardened, its better if they are already portioned and return then in the freezer.

When you need to use them, directly boil them from frozen in the boiling water and proceed per the recipe.

ADVICE

If you desire to impress your guests with a special effect, Cuttlefish offers it on a silver platter. The black cuttlefish is the one you can find in the well-stocked fishmongers. It can be used instead of a tomato by dissolving few tablespoons in hot water or dilute it in a couple of tablespoons for a more full-bodied sauce. Add it directly to fresh pasta for a total black effect.

Pasta with Zucchini and Shrimp

Prep time: 10 minutes

Cook time: 24 minutes

Serves: 4

Difficulty: Low

Cost: Low

Ingredients:

- 320 g semolina pasta, durum wheat

- Extra virgin olive oil

- 1 garlic clove

- 2 courgettis

- ½ white wine glass

- 200 g shelled shrimps

- 1 sprig Parsley

- 1 onion

Preparation:

1. Wash the onion and chop them into rings. Wash the courgettis and slice them. In running tap water, wash the peeled shrimp. Cut the garlic clove into two and chop one piece. Wash the parsley and chop them too and put them together with the garlic.

2. Make the dressing: add 2 tbsp virgin oil to a nonstick pan and add in the onion. Fry them for about 2 minutes and then add in the courgettes. Sauté for about 9 minutes. Pour in the shrimp, salt and stir. Add some white wine and cook for about 9 minutes.

3. Prepare the pasta. Add salted water to a pot and bring to boil. Add in the pasta and cook al dente as per the package instructions.

4. Drain the pasta and put it in a pan with the shrimps and courgettes. Cook for about 3-4 minutes while constantly stirring. Turn the heat off and finish with the recipe. Serve and enjoy.

STORAGE

It is advised that you eat immediately and not store.

ADVICE

Always use fresh shrimp as it will give more flavor.

Garganelli con Pesto di Zucchine e Gamberetti (Garganelli with Zucchini Pesto and Shrimp)

Prep time: 20 minutes

Serves: 4

Difficulty: Very easy

Cost: Low

Ingredients:

For pasta

- 400 g egg Garganelli

For the zucchini pesto

- 30 g pine nuts

- 200 g Zucchini

- 125 g Extra virgin olive oil

- 10 g Basil

- 30 g Pecorino, grated

- 30 g Parmesan cheese

- 2 g Salt

For sautéed shrimp

- 1 Garlic clove

- 30 g Extra virgin olive oil

- 250 g Shrimp

- 1 pinch, Salt

Preparation:

1. Wash the courgettis and remove the ends and using a large mesh grater, grate them. Put the zucchini that has been grated in a colander in order for them to lose the excess liquid and lightly salt them.

2. Gently clean the mixer using a dry cloth then put the pine nuts, basil leaves, courgettis, pecorino and the grated parmesan and lastly pour in the extra virgin olive oil.

3. Blend all together until you obtain a creamy consistency. Set aside after adding a pinch of salt.

4. For the shrimp, use the knife to cut the back along its entire length and use a tip to pull away the intestine.

5. Get a non-stick pan and pour in extra virgin olive oil and fry the garlic clove until brown. Once its brown, remove the garlic and add the shrimp. Over medium heat, sauté them for 5 minutes until they form a crispy crust on the outside.

6. Boil a pot of salted water and cook the Garganelli, drain them and finish the cooking with the shrimp together.

7. Take the Garganelli to the pan where the prawns were cooked. Add a ladle of cooking water and cook together for 1 minute. And lastly add the courgette pesto to the fire.

8. Mix everything well so that the pasta and the dressing can mix nicely. Your Garganelli with zucchini pesto and shrimp are now ready. Serve and enjoy.

STORAGE

Garganelli with courgette pesto and shrimp can be stored in the refrigerator for 1-day maximum when closed tightly in a container.

Zucchini pesto can be kept in a refrigerator for 1-2 days if it's in a small glass container and is covered with a drizzle of oil.

It's not recommended to freeze.

ADVICE

You can enrich the courgette pesto with almonds if you prefer and add courgette slices to the pasta to be sautéed with the shrimp in the pan.

However, for a note of color, cherry tomatoes are perfect.

Spaghetti with Seafood

Prep time: 35 minutes

Cook time: 20 minutes

Serves: 4

Difficulty: Medium

Cost: High

Ingredients:

- 1 kg Mussels
- 300 g Squid
- 320 g Spaghetti
- 1 kg Clams
- 8 Scampi
- 4 tbsp Extra virgin olive oil
- 1 sprig Parsley to be chopped
- 300 g Cherry tomatoes
- 1 Garlic clove
- Salt to taste
- Black pepper to taste

- 40 g White wine

Preparation:

1. In preparing spaghetti with seafood, begin with cleaning the clams and mussels and then put a colander in a container in order for it not to torch the bottom and then fill it with running water and let the clams release the excess sand drain.

2. Pour the water and then repeat the operation and leave them to soak. Go to cleaning the mussels. On the valves, remove all the impurities that are there using the back of the blade and if they are very resistant, tear away the fine linen (the beard part which comes out) and then use a new steel wool to grate away all impurities.

3. You should beat the shell firmly but not with so much force to see if the shell of the clams only contain sand. After cutting it downwards and you notice a black spot on the cutting board, just discard it because that means that it filled with sand. You can as well use a knife to cut in order to confirm if it contains sand.

4. In a large pan, heat 2 tablespoons of olive oil and once it is hot, pour in the mussels and clams and use a lid to cover

immediately. Wait until they are completely open. This will take between 3-4 minutes.

5. Remove the lid once the clams and mussels are open and pour them in a container. To eliminate any sand residues and impurities, do not throw the cooking liquid away but use a narrow mesh strainer to filter it and keep it warm. Shell both the mussels and clams and keep some other shells and mussels still full while you remove the empty shells.

6. You can dedicate yourself to squid cleaning if you don't use them when already cleaned. You will have to remove the entrails and the head, then you remove the skin and then only engrave the surface part, your can do so by entering in its interior with the blade until it completely opens and then cut it into strips.

7. Now go to cleaning the prawns. Using scissors, remove the armor that covers the abdomen by cutting the sides of the tail. To remove the intestine, the black fillet present in the Norway Lobster, use a toothpick. You won't release a bitter taste in such a way. Now you can wash the cherry tomatoes and cut them into wedges.

8. In the meantime, on the fire, put a pan full of salty water and bring it to boil. This will be used to cook spaghetti. In a pan, flavor 25 g of extra virgin olive oil with a garlic clove and once its browned, pour the squid with a pinch of salt and cook them for 5 minutes then you blend them with white wine.

9. Remove the garlic and add cherry tomatoes once the alcohol evaporates and cook for another 5 minutes. In the meantime, cook the spaghetti in boiling water.

10. To the sauce, add the salt, pepper and scampi. In a pan, directly drain the spaghetti when 4 minutes are left after the cooking. Keep cooking by pouring the cooking water that is necessary for the clams and mussels that you kept aside.

11. In the end, add the shelled clams and mussels. Turn off the heat once the cooking is ended. Use the chopped parsley to season and then mix one more time.

12. Serve your hot spaghetti.

STORAGE

It's advisable to consume the spaghetti with seafood immediately.

You can keep it in a glass container covered with a plastic wrap in a refrigerator for a maximum of 1 day.

It's not recommended to freeze

ADVICE

To give it a more aromatic note, you can replace the wine with cognac or brandy. To enrich the aroma and taste, add a little chili pepper. A pinch of spicy won't hurt.

Pappardelle agli Asparagi e Gamberi

(Pappardelle with Asparagus and Prawns)

Prep time: 20 minutes

Cook time: 20 minutes

Serves: 4

Difficulty: Easy

Cost: Medium

Ingredients:

- 250 g Egg pappardelle

- 400 g Asparagus

- 30 g Butter

- 60 g White wine

- 200 g Peeled tails prawns

- 100 g Fresh liquid cream

- 1 Small golden onion

- Salt to taste

- 2 tbsp Chopped chives

- Black pepper to taste

Preparation:

1. In preparation of the pappardelle with asparagus and shrimp, begin by cleaning the asparagus. Cut the base away and peel the lighter and leatherier part.

2. In a special asparagera, boil the whole asparagus for 5-10 minutes while keeping the tips out of the water. You should not prolong the cooking in order not to undo the asparagus, which must maintain a certain consistency. You will have to adjust to the asparagus size in such a case.

3. Remove the asparagus from the pan and then cut half into 4 slices and keep the tips. To create the sauce, use the other half of the asparagus. Use a mixer to blend them with a ladle of cooking water until a creamy mixture is got.

4. Meanwhile, chop the onion finely and in a non0stick pan, melt 30 g of butter, pour in the chopped onions and dry for 3 minutes on heat that is moderate. For the meantime, put on the fire a pan full of salty water and bring it to boil, this water will be used to cook the pasta.

5. Add the shelled prawn tails and cook for few minutes and then add the white wine. Allow it to evaporate and add the asparagus into slices.

6. Combine together the sauce and cream, pepper and salt to taste and over moderate heat, continue cooking. Meanwhile cook the pasta for like 4 minutes or for the time that is indicated on the package.

7. You can now drain the pasta keeping the cooking water aside. In the pan, pour the pappardelle with the sauce, add asparagus tips and keep aside. Saute them for few minutes and if necessary, be adding cooking water.

8. Lastly, flavor the chopped chives. Now the pappardelle with asparagus and prawns are ready to be served hot.

STORAGE

You can keep the pappardelle with asparagus and prawns for a couple of days in an airtight container in a refrigerator. Its not advisable to freeze.

ADVICE

Use fish broth to flavor the dish instead of cream and for the sauté, replace the butter with olive oil if you want to prepare a lighter version.

Chapter 6: Baked Pasta

Lasagna

Prep time: 30 minutes

Cook time: 25 minutes

Serves: 8

Difficulty: Medium

Cost: Medium

Ingredients:

For a 20x30 cm baking tray

- 250 g Parmesan cheese DOP to be grated

- 21 Green Lasagna with egg puffs

For the Bolognese sauce

- 50 g Carrots

- 500 g Chopped beef pulp

- 250 g Tomato sauce

- 50 g Celery

- 250 g Ground pork, very fatty

- 50 g Onions

- 3 l water

- 1 tbsp Extra virgin olive oil

- Black pepper to taste

- 40 g Whole milk

- Salt to taste

- 250 g White wine

For the bechamel

- 100 g 00 flour

- Nutmeg to taste

- 100 g Butter

- Salt

- 1 l Fresh whole milk

Preparation:

1. Chop the celery finely. Peel the onions and carrots and get 50 g of each.

2. Add oil in a pan and heat it. Add the veggies and cook while occasionally stirring for about 10 minutes. Add minced pork and ground beef.

3. Cook the meat slowly for 10 minutes until it is brown as you stir occasionally. When the juices come out and white wine and blend. When the wine evaporates fully, add in tomato sauce and 1 liter of water.

4. Add salt and mix. Cook on medium heat for 60 minutes. Add another liter of water after 60 minutes and stir. Cook for 60 more minutes and add in the last liter of water and cook on low heat. After the 3 hours, the ragu should be thick but not too dry. Add pepper and salt to season, turn the heat off, pour in milk and stir. Set it aside.

5. Make the béchamel: heat milk in a saucepan. In the meantime, melt butter on low heat in small pieces in a different pan. When melted, remove from the stove. Add

flour and stir thoroughly using a whisk. Stir until there is no lump left in the mixture. Return the pan back to the heat and heat it on low heat to brown it.

6. When the milk boils, add grated nutmeg to flavor it. Add salt too. Mix it with the flour and butter mixture. Use a hand whisk to vigorously mix the ingredients and then put on low heat to thicken it: it should be lump-free and homogenous. Cook on low heat for about 7 minutes until it becomes creamy.

7. Get a baking dish rectangular in shape (30x20 cm) and drizzle béchamel on it. Spread on the surface ensuring it is even and lay the lasagna mix. Add another béchamel layer and another layer of grated Parmesan and ragu. Ensure that the whole pan is evenly covered.

8. Create another lasagna layer followed by another béchamel layer. Spread it evenly. Add ragu and proceed to make the layers alternating Parmesan, ragù, bechamel, and green sheets.

9. Have a rag layer on top and put lots of parmesan. When the pan is ready, bake in an oven that has been preheated for 25 minutes at 200 °. As soon as the crust turns golden,

know the lasagna is ready. Remove from oven and put on a table to cool them before you taste.

STORAGE

Put the sauce in an airtight container and store it in the fridge for up to 3 days. To freeze it, you need to use fresh ingredients to cook. To cook, put in a fridge to defrost for 24 hours and put in an oven to cook.

Pasticciata

Prep time: 20 minutes

Cook time: 1 hour 10 minutes

Serves: 6

Difficulty: Easy

Cost: Low

Ingredients:

- 800 g Tomato sauce
- 200 g Provola
- 160 g Mortadella
- 500 g Rigatoni
- 200 g Parmesan cheese DOP
- 4 Eggs
- 130 g Salami
- 130 g Mozzarella
- 1 Small onion
- 1 clove Garlic
- Salt
- Basil to taste

- Extra virgin olive oil

- Thyme to taste

Preparation:

1. Pour cold water in a pot and add in the eggs. Bring them to boil and cook for 10 minutes. When ready, remove the shells while hot and set them aside.

2. Meanwhile, make the sauce: chop garlic clove and a clean onion. Add oil to a pan on low heat and add in the garlic and onion. Sauté for 15 minutes as you add a few tbsp of water to prevent burning.

3. Add tomato sauce, salt and stir. Cook on low heat for about 32-35 minutes until the sauce is hard. Chop the basil leaves using your hands and add them. Add thyme leaves too. Use an appropriate egg cutter or a knife to slice the eggs and make sure that the slices are regular.

4. Cut the Provola, mortadella, and salami cheese into cubes. In order to reduce extra whey, put them in a colander. Bring salted water to boil and add the rigatoni to cook.

5. When halfway into cooking, drain the pasta and add it into the sauce. Use two thirds of the provola, mortadella, and salami cubes mixture to season.

6. Thoroughly mix the contents and move to a baking dish (34x24 cm). Add half the boiled eggs and 2 spoons full of parmesan.

7. Add the provola, mortadella, and salami mixture that remained and use the rest of the dough to cover.

8. Add the mozzarella and grated parmesan and the remaining eggs. Preheat your oven to 200 ° in readiness to bake the pasta. Put the pasta in the oven and bake for 15 minutes and grill for about 5 minutes so that the surface turns brown. Serve and enjoy!

STORAGE

You can store it in a fridge for up to 3 days. You can alternatively cook the following day; get it ready and cover it with a plastic wrap and put it in a refrigerator. You can also freeze it, raw or cooked.

ADVICE

You are free to modify the ingredients as per your tastes: if you love savory flavors you can use smoked bacon or if you like flavors that are delicate, sweet bacon or cooked ham are great. You can add more bechamel for more taste that is irresistible.

Sorrentina

Prep time: 15 minutes

Cook time: 45 minutes

Serves: 4

Difficulty: Easy

Cost: Low

Ingredients:

- 320 g Fusilli
- 1 Garlic clove
- 125 g Mozzarella
- 500 g Tomato sauce
- Salt to taste
- 30 g Extra virgin olive oil
- Basil to taste
- 65 g PDO grated Parmesan cheese

Preparation:

1. In preparing the Sorrento style pasta, begin by preparing the sauce. In a large pan, pour in the oil and then add the

peeled garlic clove. Pour in the tomato puree after frying for 1 minute.

2. Use salt to season and add few basil leaves and then mix. Cover using a lid and over low heat, cook for 30 minutes. Remember to remove the garlic cloves after cooking.

3. Put a pot full of water on the fire to heat. This water will be used for pasta cooking.

4. Meanwhile, take care of the mozzarella. Cut then into cubes. Once the water boils, cook the pasta and then dry it al dente in the sauce directly and stir to mix them.

5. In a 25 cm diameter baking dish, pour have of the pasta for making the first layer and add half of the mozzarella cubes. Sprinkle a little parmesan on the same. Cover with the dough that has remained and then add mozzarella and lastly cover using parmesan.

6. In the oven on grill mode, sauté for 5 minutes until the pasta is well au gratin and the mozzarella melted. You can put the pan on the highest shelf and turn the oven on maximum power if you don't have a grill. But be careful not to burn.

7. Use fresh basil to garnish your Sorrentina pasta and serve immediately.

STORAGE

It is advisable to consume while still steaming, hot and stringy. You can store it for a maximum of 2 days closed in an airtight container and kept in a fridge. If freezing is preferred, make sure you stay a behind a little with the pasta cooking.

You can also prepare everything in advance if you prefer and cook au gratin before serving. Or you can cook the sauce and at the end only prepare the pasta.

ADVICE

Prepare the sauce with good tomato sauce if you want to respect the tradition and remain on the classic. Pass them with the vegetable mill at the end of cooking.

You can also add tomato sauce like 1 tablespoon, it will be enough if you prefer a more full-bodied sauce and with a more intense taste.

You can sprinkle with breadcrumbs for a crunchier surface.

Classic Baked Pasta

Prep time: 30 minutes

Cook time: 80 minutes

Serves: 10

Difficulty: Easy

Cost: Medium

Ingredients:

For baked pasta

- 600 g Rigatoni
- 3 tbsp Parmesan cheese DOP to grate
- 300 g Scamorza provola
- 4 Medium eggs

For the meatballs

- 250 g Ground pork
- 100 g Parmesan cheese DOP to be grated
- 2 tbsp Chopped parsley
- 150 g Sausage
- Salt to taste

- 100 g Bread crumbs

- 2 Medium eggs

- 1 pinch Nutmeg

- Black pepper to taste

For the sauce

- Tomato sauce

- 4 tbsp Extra virgin olive oil

- Salt to taste

- 1 White onions

- 5 Basil leaves

- Black pepper to taste

- 1 Garlic clove

For the bechamel

- 80 g 00 flour

- 80 g Butter

- 1 l Whole milk

- 1 pinch Nutmeg

- Salt to taste

Preparation:

1. For pasta preparing in the oven, begin with the meatball's dough. Begin by taking the sausage and cutting it in half to remove the casing with surrounds it. Use a knife to chop the meat roughly.

2. Pour the minced meat in a large bowl and add the grated parmesan, chopped parsley, sausage and the breadcrumbs that were previously crumbled in a mixer.

3. Season with pepper and salt after adding the eggs. Use your hands to work on the dough until you get a homogeneous mixture. Use a plastic wrap to cover it and leave it to rest until the meatballs are prepared.

4. Now take care of the sauce. Pour the finely chopped onions, whole garlic clove and oil in a large non-stick pan. Once the oil is hot, pour in the salt, pepper and tomato puree and on low heat, cover with a lid and cook for 30 minutes occasionally stirring.

5. Meanwhile, shape meatballs of 10 g each and put them on a plate. With this amount of dough, you can get like 70 meatballs. Remove the garlic and pour the meatballs in the sauce after its cooking time is over.

6. Use pepper and salt to season and then use a spatula to mix. Over low heat, allow it to cook for 15 minutes. Add the chopped basil leaves and leave to cook for more 5 minutes.

7. Lastly, go to eggs preparation. Boil them for 10 minutes to firm them after boiling water. Under running water, cool them. Shell the hard-boiled eggs once they are cold and using a sharp knife or any other appropriate tool, cut them in slices and keep them in a small bowl aside.

8. Cut the scamorza into slice and then into strips and lastly into cubes. Set them aside after putting them in a small bowl.

9. Now go to the preparation of the bechamel. In a saucepan, heat the milk. On low heat, heat the butter into small pieces and allow it to melt in a separate pan. To the flour, add the melted butter after turning off the heat. Use a hand whisk to vigorously stir in order to avoid lumps.

10. Take the saucepan back to the heat and over low heat, cook the obtained cream until it becomes golden. You will then get a roux. Using a wire, add the hot milk and use salt and nutmeg to season.

11. On low heat, cook the bechamel for 5-6 minutes until it becomes thick. Continue mixing using a hand whisk. You can now transfer the bechamel to a bowl and then use a cling film to cover it until the time it will be used. This helps avoiding crust formation on the surface.

12. In much salted water, boil the pasta and through cooking, drain it half way. Get the readymade meatball sauce and add it to the pasta. Use a spoon to mix the ingredients well and on the bottom, of a baking dish distribute a bechamel layer and create the first layer of meatballs and rigatoni.

13. Over the dough, spread half of the diced scamorza and half the sliced boiled eggs and use half of the grated parmesan to sprinkle.

14. Use a few spoonfuls of bechamel to season the first layer and continue to the second layer of meatballs and pasta evenly distributing it over the first one. Use other sliced eggs distributed evenly on the baking dish to complete the layer.

15. Use bechamel and diced scarmorza to sprinkle. Use the remaining grated parmesan to sprinkle and over a static oven bake at 180 degrees for 15 minutes.

16. Set the oven function to grill mode after cooking and cook au gratin for 5 minutes. The basked pasta is now ready. Allow it to rest for 5-10 minutes at room temperature before you enjoy it.

STORAGE

If left over, the baked pasta can be put in a tightly closed container and frozen in the refrigerator for a maximum of 2 days.

If you sed fresh ingredients for preparing, baked pasta can be frozen, portioned or whole both cooked and low.

Complete defrosting is advisable before continuing with cooking in the oven for subsequent consumption.

ADVICE

Just before serving, you can prepare it in advance and put it in the oven. You can also prepare the meatball sauce the day before to speed up the preparation.

You can use mozzarella, cacio cavallo or other cheeses of your preference. There is no problem if the scamorza taste is too intense for you.

Cannelloni

Prep time: 1 hour 30 minutes

Cook time: 50 minutes

Serves: 5

Difficulty: Easy

Cost: Low

Ingredients:

- 3 Eggs

- 300 g 00 flour

For the tomato sauce

- 250 g Tomato sauce

- 1 Garlic clove

- 3 tbsp Extra virgin olive oil

- Salt to taste

For the bechamel

- 25 g Butter

- Grated nutmeg to taste

- 250 g Whole milk

- 25 g 00 flour

- Salt up to a pinch

- 1 pinch Ground black pepper

For the stuffing

- 200 g Sausage

- 100 g Parmesan cheese DOP to be grated

- 2 Medium eggs

- 300 g Ground beef

- 80 g Onions

- 80 g Carrots

- 10 g Extra virgin olive oil

- 20 g Red wine

- 60 g Celery

- Black pepper 1 pinch

- Salt up to a pinch

To sprinkle

- 15 g Parmesan cheese DOP to be grated

Preparation:

1. For preparing the cannelloni, begin by preparing the egg pasta. In a large bowl, pour in the previously beaten eggs and the flour.

2. Use your hands to knead until you get a rather uniform mixture. Transfer the mixture on the work surface and work on it until you get smooth dough that you will give a spherical shape. Use a plastic wrap to wrap it and leave it to rest for 1 hour.

3. Meanwhile take care on making the simple sauce. In a pan, pour a drizzle of oil and add garlic. Pour in the tomato puree, pepper and salt after it browns. Use a lid to cover and on a moderate heat, let it cook for 30 minutes occasionally stirring.

4. In this period, also make the bechamel. In a pan, pour in the butter and allow it to melt. Add the sieved flour and use a whisk to quickly mix. Pour in the hot milk and keep stirring once you get a slightly brown roux.

5. Use pepper and salt to season and add the grated nutmeg. Allow the bechamel to thicken and keep mixing it. Pour it in a glass bowl and use a contact film to cover.

6. Now, prepare the filling. Finely chop the onions, celery and carrot and prepare the sauté. Transfer them onto a pan with a drizzle of oil and add minced meat. Crumble the sausage with your hands after removing it from its casing.

7. In the pan, add the sausage and stir often until everything browns. Add pepper and salt and when the meat has changed color, add the red wine. Pour everything in a glass bowl once they have cooked for at least 10 minutes.

8. Add the grated parmesan and eggs when the meat has cooled and mix everything well. Your egg pasta will have rested at this point. Take the dough back and divide it in half and with the help of a dough sheeter, spread the two halves and get a thickness of about 1-2 mm and cut rectangles with dimensions of 14x9 cm from every sheet.

9. Blanch a rectangle of pasta for 1 minute each at a time in much slightly salted boiling water and transfer them to the tray. Where you will have put a clean cloth. You can pass them in cold water for a moment if you want in order to block cooking but the most crucial part is laying out different rectangles perfectly minus over lapping them.

10. Now take care of the cannelloni stuffing. On the shorter part of the rectangle, put some filling and use wet hands to

roll them. Spread a little bechamel and few spoonsful of the sauce on the pan bottom once the cannelloni are rolled up and lay the cannelloni side by side.

11. Use the bechamel leftovers and sauce to cover the cannelloni surface and use grated parmesan to sprinkle the surface.

12. In a preheated static oven, bake for 15 minutes at 180 degrees and using the grill function, bake for 3 minutes. Once fully baked, serve your cannelloni while still hot.

STORAGE

You can use a refrigerator to store your cannelloni, close it in an airtight container for 1-2 days maximum.

You can freeze them incase you had used all fresh ingredients.

ADVICE

You can pour a mixture of eggs and meat in a piping bag to facilitate the filling of your cannelloni. This will make it easier to arrange the filling on different puff pastry rectangles.

Lasagne alla Norma

Prep time: 20 minutes

Cook time: 45 minutes

Serves: 6

Difficulty: Easy

Ingredients:

- 1 garlic clove
- 6 basil leaves
- 250 g egg Lasagne
- Extra virgin olive oil
- 500 g eggplants
- Salted ricotta
- 1 kg peeled tomatoes
- Black pepper
- Salt

For the ricotta cream

- Nutmeg
- 200 ml whole milk
- 1 kg cow's milk ricotta

- Salt and black pepper to taste

Preparation

1. Making the Lasagne alla Norma, begin by preparing the tomato sauce, heat the oil and cook a garlic clove. Pour the salt, pepper and tomato puree in the pan and cook the sauce. When you finish cooking, turn off the heat and set aside and season with basil leaves.

2. Wash and pee; the auberges, cut them to get slices of 1 centimeter thick using a mandolin. Heat the pan and blush it with some oil and grill the auberge slices until they turn golden on both sides. Allow them to cool and then slice them into cubes.

Now go to preparing the ricotta cream.

1. Dilute the ricotta with milk and mix the whisk to get a homogeneous and soft mixture. Add pepper and salt and sprinkle with nutmeg as a flavor.

2. Lastly grate the salted ricotta. Everything is now ready for making the Lasagne at this point. Take an oven proof dish, season with oil and spread a tomato sauce layer. Put the first layer of Lasagne, add a layer of tomato, the ricotta cream, diced auberges, sprinkle the grated salted ricotta and continue alternating the layers with another row of

sheets until you have used up all the ingredients. End with a layer of salted ricotta and auberges.

3. Bake for 20 minutes in a preheated static oven at 220 degrees.

4. Once cooked, remove your Lasagne alla Norma and enjoy.

STORAGE

You can cover the Lasagne alla Norma in an airtight container or with a cling film and store in the refrigerator for 1-2 days.

You can prepare them the day before and cover them with a plastic wrap, keep them in a refrigerator and cook them the next day.

If you have used all fresh ingredients, preferably if they are raw, it is possible to freeze them.

If you want to cook them in the oven, just defrost them before in the refrigerator for 24 hours.

ADVICE

If you want a better and richer taste, instead of grilling the auberges, you can fry them in seed oil.

Gnocchi alla Romana

Prep time: 15 minutes

Cook time: 35 minutes

Serves: 5

Difficulty: Medium

Cost: Low

Ingredients:

- 100 g Butter
- 2 yolks
- 1 l whole milk
- 250 g Semolina
- 40 g Pecorino
- Nutmeg
- 100 g Parmesan cheese, Grated
- 7 g Salt

Preparation:

1. Preparing the gnocchi alla Romana, put the milk in a pan on the stove and add a knob of butter like 30 g of the whole dose, a pinch of nutmeg and salt and as soon as it begins boiling, pour the semolina in the rain and use a whisk to stir vigorously to avoid formation of lumps.

2. On low heat, cook the mixture for few minutes and when it thickens, remove the pan from heat and add two yolks to this mixture and use a wooden spoon to mix. Add parmesan and mix again. At this time, pour on the sheet of parchment paper, half of the still boiling dough and give it a cylindrical shape using your hands.

3. You can pass your hands under cold water in order not to get too hot. Wrap the obtained uniform cylinder in a parchment paper. Let the same operation be repeated for the second half of the dough that was kept aside and place two rolls in a fridge for 20 minutes.

4. You will get compact dough and with the use of a knife, you will be able to obtain perfect discs once cooled. We recommend moistening with water to facilitate cutting.

5. On the previously buttered baking sheet, arrange the obtained 40 pieces and sprinkle them with melted butter like 70 g but not boiling.

6. Bake in a preheated static oven for 20-25 minutes at 200 degrees after sprinkling the surface with pecorino Romana. Activate the grill function and allow them to cook au gratin for 5 minutes.

7. When ready, serve your gnocchi alla Romana while still hot.

STORAGE

Keep the gnocchi all Romana for up to 2 days in a container in a hermetically sealed refrigerator.

You can as well season the gnocchi all Romana with butter and cheese in bowls and freeze it and directly pass them in the oven without defrosting them instead of melting.

ADVICE

Add few sage leaves between one dumpling and another to further enhance the taste of the dumplings

Conclusion

The art of making pasta has a history of hundreds of years, do not expect to make masterpieces at the first attempt but continue to practice cooking even more delicious pasta dishes.

I hope you have discovered a few helpful tips to making these sauces and making them as delicious as possible. Making your own delicious pasta sauce recipes can make any Italian dish mouthwatering and better.

So, what is next for you? The next step for you to make is to begin making all of these delicious pasta sauces for yourself. Once you have done that begin making your own sauce recipes from scratch by utilizing all of the ingredients you have used in the dishes in this book.

CPSIA information can be obtained
at www.ICGtesting.com
Printed in the USA
BVHW010917180221
R11879400001B/R118794PG599628BVX00071B/34

9 781801 740128